50 Hikes

FOR Eastern Washington's
Highest Mountains

James P. Johnson

50 Hikes
FOR Eastern Washington's
Highest Mountains

James P. Johnson

Frank
Amato
PORTLAND

Dedication

*To my mother and father who gave me
the freedom to explore.*

Acknowledgments

*I'd like to thank George McNicholl and John Ogmundson of the
U.S. Forest Service for their assistance. Thanks to Bruce Howard
and Carl Berg for helpful comments and suggestions. A very
special thank you to Nancy Correll whose work on the
maps made this book possible.*

Cover Photos:

North Baldy • Gypsy Peak

Grizzly Mountain

© 2003 James P. Johnson

Frank Amato Publications, Inc.

P.O. Box 82112, Portland, Oregon 97282

503.653.8108 • www.amatobooks.com

All photographs by the author unless otherwise noted.

Map Illustrations: Nancy Correll

Book & Cover Design: Kathy Johnson

Printed in Singapore

Softbound ISBN: 1-57188-296-0 • UPC: 0-81127-00126-2

1 3 5 7 9 10 8 6 4 2

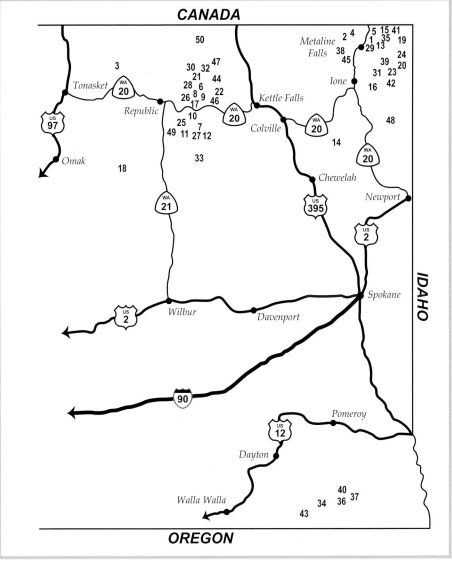

1. **Gypsy Peak**
2. **Abercrombie Mountain**
3. **Mount Bonaparte**
4. **Hooknose Mountain**
5. **South Fork**
6. **Copper Butte**
7. **Snow Peak**
8. **Scar Mountain**
9. **Wapaloosie Mountain**
10. **Sherman Peak**
11. **Bald Mountain**
12. **White Mountain**
13. **Crowell Ridge**
14. **Calispell Peak**
15. **Salmo Mountain**
16. **Molybdenite Mountain**
17. **Columbia Mountain**

18. **Moses Mountain**
19. **Shedroof Mountain**
20. **Helmer Mountain**
21. **Midnight Mountain**
22. **King Mountain**
23. **Mankato Mountain**
24. **Thunder Mountain**
25. **Edds Mountain**
26. **Jungle Hill**
27. **Barnaby Buttes**
28. **Lambert Mountain**
29. **Sullivan Mountain**
30. **Mount Leona**
31. **Roundtop Mountain**
32. **Profanity Peak**
33. **Grizzly Mountain**
34. **Oregon Butte**

35. **Leola Peak**
36. **Diamond Peak**
37. **Mount Misery**
38. **Sherlock Peak**
39. **Hall Mountain**
40. **West Butte**
41. **Prouty Peak**
42. **Grassy Top Mountain**
43. **Table Rock**
44. **U S Mountain**
45. **Linton Mountain**
46. **Mack Mountain**
47. **Taylor Ridge**
48. **North Baldy Mountain**
49. **Seventeenmile Mountain**
50. **Togo Mountain**

KATHY JOHNSON

Contents

KATHY JOHNSON

Introduction

They aren't world famous, nor will you see them pictured in the Sierra Club calendar. Nevertheless, Eastern Washington's highest fifty mountains are beautiful and awe-inspiring.

Some are bare rock peaks jutting steeply skyward, climbable only by hand-to-rock scrambling over boulder fields and rocky slopes. Others are gently-inclined, tree-capped summits up which small children can walk.

But one of the best things about the highest mountains in Eastern Washington is that they are practically ignored. Relatively few people experience the landscape of Eastern Washington's high country, and that means uncrowded trails and plenty of solitude.

Our proximity to well-known hiking areas in the Cascades, the B.C. Selkirks, the Wallowas of northeastern Oregon, and the Idaho and Montana Rockies means the backcountry of our area is often overlooked. While the scenery of the above places is hard to beat, there are areas of Eastern Washington with stunning, mountainous terrain that rivals the prominent ranges that neighbor us.

Another great thing about Eastern Washington's fifty highest mountains is that one doesn't have to be a mountain climber to reach the top. Any hiker possessing a little ambition and the physical condition to walk a few hilly miles can climb each mountain on the list without need of technical skill or equipment.

In addition, every mountain on the list can be climbed as a day hike. Of course, hiking time will vary—a few mountains can be done in as little as an hour or less, while a handful are full-day, early-morning to evening treks. If you're the ambitious type, some mountains are clustered enough that you can climb two or more in a single day.

A few hikers may snicker at the idea of composing a list of Eastern Washington mountains. The higher, more rugged peaks of the previously mentioned ranges may make our local mountains seem unappealing to some. However, there are compelling reasons why hikers would choose to climb in Eastern Washington rather than the more well-known ranges.

As mentioned earlier, trails that lead to Eastern Washington summits are uncrowded. It's entirely possible to hike a mountain on a beautiful summer weekend and encounter no one along the way. The light use means there's no limits on hikers, no permit requirements, and no fees in almost all areas, (a few trailheads require a valid Northwest Forest Pass).

Because sheer rock faces, plunging cliffs, and pinnacles are less common, hikers don't face great danger or difficulty in reaching the summits of Eastern Washington mountains. There's less danger of rockfall or slides, and the warmer summers and drier climate of the Inland Northwest mean quicker snow melt and earlier access to the high country.

For the Eastern Washington resident, hiking this area's mountains allows you to know your own backyard a little better. It also allows a more frequent dose of mountain scenery for people who thrive on the grandeur of nature. Those who only have time for a once-a-year backpacking trip to a favorite but distant hiking area can do day-trips that require much less time, planning, and organizing. No matter where in Eastern Washington one lives, it's possible to go out the front door in the morning, conquer a mountain, and be back home for dinner.

One downside, though not limited to Eastern Washington, is the lack of respect shown to our forests by timber managers. Though numerous mountains on the highest 50 list are protected within wilderness areas, many are not and several are managed primarily for resource extraction, not recreation.

A young hiker takes in the view atop Diamond Peak in the Blue Mountains of southeast Washington.

There are a few mountains where you'll come across landscapes that are eerily similar to a battlefield. Heavy logging has left a landscape devoid of trees and so torn up that bombs couldn't have done a better job ripping up the land. Such treatment of the earth brings about a sense of anger and injustice. Hikers are likely to sense the lack of reverence and overemphasis on taking without respect to the natural processes that give us this resource.

It's beneficial for people to get out and see what's being done in our forests for it can lead to more careful and considerate harvesting. However for now, hikers will have to tolerate these unsightly areas and hope that the future will bring a change for the better.

It's always a thrill to climb a mountain and enjoy the view from the top, however, it's just one part of the grand experience of being outside, far removed from house or car, reduced to our most basic relationship with the natural world. Simply pausing to examine a rock outcrop along a trail, looking up the huge, arrow-straight trunk of an old ponderosa, or while sitting on a rock and enjoying a snack, noticing how the arrangement of bushes, trees, and fallen timber make a scene so perfect and beautiful that no artist could have done better. Small things like this stir the emotions and heighten our sense of wonder and humility, bringing happiness and a satisfaction for being alive. Often, these scenes stay in the mind for days and in a restful or unoccupied moment, they suddenly click into view, bringing back the same emotional response as the original experience.

Although the goal of the 50 hikes described in this book is to reach the summit of a mountain, it's the whole journey from trailhead to mountaintop that provides the enjoyment. So take your time, looking, listening, and contemplating as you work your way up the slopes. Let the many aspects of the natural world reach and infect you with its grandeur, its calmness and beauty. Allow yourself to be rewarded and awed as you enjoy the view from the top of Eastern Washington's highest places.

Determining the Highest 50 Mountains

Before a list of the highest peaks on this side of the state could be compiled, the boundaries of Eastern Washington first had to be defined. Looking at almost any map of Washington, there's an obvious natural division that cuts the state into two roughly equal halves and is also a low point from which the land rises going both east and west. This dividing line is the Columbia River valley, from its southernmost point where it first forms the border with Oregon, upstream to its confluence with the Okanogan River, and northward along that river to the Canadian border. Thus the entire Cascade Range is considered to be in the western half of the state, and none of its peaks are included on the list.

Because there exists no official list of the highest peaks in Eastern Washington, a thorough search of USGS topographic maps was undertaken. But the more difficult task was establishing the criteria in deciding what constitutes a mountain.

As many hikers and climbers know, there's a big gray area when it comes to applying the term *mountain*. Land masses that rise far above the surrounding landscape, standing alone, are easy to pick out and call a mountain. Often is the case, however, when a long, high ridge topped by several peaks makes this determination more difficult. Is every pinnacle or high point a mountain, even if some are separated by only a couple hundred feet? Or is the entire ridge one mountain, even if there are plunging valleys between peaks and the ridge is many miles long?

A variety of standards have been devised to solve these questions, all of which have their shortcomings, and none of which have been adopted universally.

One standard states there must be a certain mileage between peaks. Two peaks inside the mileage standard are considered one peak. However, the shortcoming with this method, besides being arbitrary, is that if all peaks along a ridge are in close proximity, each negates the neighboring peak, leaving only the highest point of the ridge considered a mountain.

Another standard states that a peak must rise a certain distance above the ridge of which it is a part. In this case, only distinct and prominent peaks along a ridge are recognized. With this standard however, there could be a very high-elevation peak, even higher than any stand-alone mountain, but if it doesn't rise far enough above the ridge, it's not considered a mountain.

A third standard, which seems to be the best method to deal with this problem, involves the elevation difference between peaks and saddles. If two peaks are connected by a ridge, the low point between the two (the saddle) must have a certain elevation difference between it and the lower-elevation peak. If this standard is met, the two peaks are separate and distinct. If it is not met, then the lower-elevation peak is considered part of the higher one.

The problem with this method is determining how much of an elevation difference must exist. Should it be 200 feet? 500 feet? A thousand or more? Any amount seems arbitrary and would surely be a source of disagreement.

After careful consideration of these standards, it was decided a system that already exists suffices quite nicely—placenames established by the U.S. Geological Survey. Therefore, any named point, be it called a mountain, ridge, or hill, is on the list if it is one of the highest 50 places.

How To Use This Book

Each hike described in this book begins with a general description of the mountain along with its highlights and interesting facts. This is followed by detailed directions for reaching the trailhead. A nearby town, easily found on a road map, has been chosen as the starting-off point for reaching the trailhead.

Because mileage is given between every turn or fork from the starting-off point to the trailhead, as well as a physical description of junctions and turns, the directions may seem long or unnecessarily detailed. However, precise directions seemed important, especially considering that some trailheads aren't really trailheads, but rather a spot along a road, unmarked by sign or obvious feature.

Many hikers have also had the experience of searching for a trailhead with a guide that inadequately described the way, and instead of hiking, the day was spent driving over a maze of dirt roads, trying to guess where the trailhead was. Directions to the trailhead were written with these experiences in mind.

Also, most of the mileages listed come from a vehicle odometer, which is believed to be fairly accurate. However, your vehicle's odometer reading may vary slightly. Relying on a combination of physical description and mileage should enable you to easily find the trailhead.

By midsummer the snow has melted in the high country leaving a lush landscape filled with wildflowers.

Many of the hikes in this book begin at major trailheads along main highways or Forest Service roads. These will always be easy to reach. A few are more remote however, involving long drives over secondary and branch roads. Over time, it's possible that road-building, logging operations, or road closures may alter the route to the trailhead. Signs which used to point the way may be knocked over or vandalized. While it's likely you won't have problems gaining access to trailheads, it's possible the route or its signage may change slightly from that described in the book.

Over the four-year span it took to hike Eastern Washington's 50 highest mountains, (and all were hiked, many of them multiple times) a four-door family sedan, definitely not designed for the back country, was used. So you don't have to own a high-clearance, four-wheel-drive vehicle to access the trailheads. However, if you drive an expensive, luxury sedan that you highly prize, you should probably leave it at home. The worst sections of road are negotiable, though you have to pick your way carefully or you'll scrape bottom. In a few places, thick brush at the roadside will scrape against your car.

When the road conditions are poor, it's mentioned in the "Getting There section."

A couple trailheads can be accessed only by high-clearance vehicles. In these cases you'll have to park short of the trailhead and walk an extra mile or two at most. These too are mentioned in the "Getting There" section.

Though some trailheads are located adjacent to a paved road, the vast majority involve a little to a great deal of gravel and dirt-road driving. The approximate mileage is mentioned for each hike. During any stretch of dry, warm weather, expect clouds of dust to smother your car as you drive to the trailhead.

Also, because some Forest Service roads aren't heavily used, you may encounter fallen trees, especially early in the season. It's a good idea to put a saw in the trunk just in case.

"The Trail" section describes the route you'll follow to climb each mountain. Though a bare majority of the mountains are reachable by trail all the way to the summit, many require a short off-trail hike to reach the top. A few require lengthy off-trail hikes.

The mileage and hiking time listed for each hike is an estimate in most cases. It assumes a moderate pace with short breaks going up, and time to take in the scenery and enjoy a snack at the summit.

In most cases, the elevation gain between the trailhead and summit isn't much different than the total elevation gain you'll experience on the hike. However, there are a few long hikes in which the total gain is significantly greater than the elevation difference between trailhead and summit. Such cases are mentioned in "The Trail section."

Though the name of the USGS 7.5 minute topographic map that covers each hike is listed, most hikers will find these maps unnecessary. However, if you plan to explore an area beyond that described in this book, topographic maps are useful, if not for keeping from getting lost, then as a fun activity locating prominent points and finding their representation on the map.

Each hike is rated according to the level of exertion needed to reach the summit.

Easy: The elevation gain is relatively mild, the hiking route allows easy walking, and isn't overly steep, nor lengthy. Anyone that is physically active can easily handle the hike.

Break a Sweat: Hiking distance and elevation gain are moderate. The route is clear, and little off-trail hiking is required. But there are steep sections that may cause you to break into a sweat.

Huffin' & Puffin': Mileage is moderate, but you're in for some very steep climbing, and possibly a lot of it. There may be some off-trail hiking required, or the trail is in poor condition in places.

Major Workout: The climb is very steep and long. Trail conditions are poor or there's lengthy off-trail hik-

ing required. A full day of hiking may be needed to reach the summit.

The final section contains notes on what can be seen from the summit. Nearby peaks are identified as well as towns, lakes, or any visible prominent feature.

Additional Information

District Ranger Stations: Each hike lists the ranger district that oversees the area. On page 118 you'll find the address and phone number for each ranger station.

For those living in the Spokane area, there's a Forest Service office on Fancher Road which supplies general information. For specific information about individual hikes, such as whether the trails are snow-free, access roads have been cleared, or stormy weather has caused road closures, the district ranger stations are always the most knowledgeable. In the smaller districts, the person that answers the phone can often provide the information you need.

Hiking Season: Depending on the depth of the snowpack and how warm it is in spring, the trails to Eastern Washington summits become snow-free anytime from the end of May to early July. The snowpack returns in late October to early November.

The Salmo-Priest Wilderness in the northeast corner of our state has the heaviest precipitation of any area in Washington east of the Cascades. Expect snow to cover the highest and shadiest areas at least through the end of June.

Bugs: One of the biggest detriments to an enjoyable hike is the presence of bugs. In the high country, mosquitoes are present from the beginning of the hiking season to mid-August.

Worse than mosquitoes are the black flies that deliver a bite which leaves a noticeable open sore and itches for days. Because their population also dwindles around mid-August, hiking becomes pleasant in late summer, and by fall, it can be virtually bug-free. Any earlier, it's a good idea to bring along bug repellent.

Ferocious Animals: Though some people harbor thoughts of large predators lurking beside trails waiting for scrumptious humans to amble along, being attacked and eaten should be low on your list of worries. Reports of hikers being injured by a wild animal attack in Eastern Washington are virtually nonexistent.

Changes in hunting laws the past few years have reportedly caused an increase in bear and cougar populations, and there have been recent incidents of immature cougars stalking or attacking small children. Even though the risk of such an attack is very low, if you bring young children along, it's a good idea to make sure they're always close to adults.

Black bears, the most common bear found in Eastern Washington forests, are naturally fearful of man. These bears will high-tail it the moment they detect a human presence.

Though it's rare that you'll encounter a bear while hiking, you'll increase your chances if you travel through high-country huckleberry patches in late summer. Hiking above 6,000 feet elevation one August in the Salmo-Priest Wilderness Area, this writer crossed paths with bears on three separate occasions in one day. In all three instances the bears fled as if their lives depended on it.

There have been newspaper accounts of grizzly bears attacking humans in places such as Glacier or Yellowstone National Park. The northeast corner of Washington is known grizzly bear habitat. Though the grizzly population is unknown, it's believed to be very small. A Forest Service employee with more than 20 years experience working in the forests and on trails in the Salmo-Priest Wilderness told this writer that he has yet to see a grizzly.

This knowledge, along with a lack of reported bear attacks, convinces many hikers that there's no need to carry a weapon or instrument for self-defense. Not once over hundreds of miles of trail and off-trail hiking was this hiker threatened by, had an encounter with, or was able to even catch sight of a grizzly bear.

However, there's always a remote possibility of running into one. Taking defensive measures such as traveling in a group or making plenty of noise while hiking can help. Some outdoor equipment stores sell pepper spray to deter charging bears. But one should decide beforehand what measures to take so that the hike is an activity of enjoyment, not fearfulness.

Trail Fees: As of the writing of this book, a few trailheads require the display of a Northwest Forest Pass. This pass, good for all fee sites in Washington and Oregon, is $30.00 per year or $5.00 for a day pass. The pass can be purchased at any Forest Service office and many businesses. To purchase or to obtain a list of businesses that sell them, call 1-800-270-7504 or go on-line at www.naturenw.org.

Hiking Party Size and Stock Use: In the Wenaha-Tucannon Wilderness, there is a party limit of 18 eyes. Any combination of stock animals and people totaling 18 eyes is the maximum. At other Eastern Washington forests there is no limit on party size or stock use.

Trail Maintenance Program: In response to a lack of funding for trailwork, the Forest Service has started a program for volunteers who are interested in combining their hobbies with a little work. Interested groups, families, or even individuals can help clear trails in the spring and early summer by performing light maintenance such as clearing downed trees and trimming overgrown brush.

If you enjoy the camaraderie of working with a group of friends or co-workers, what better way to enjoy a nice day outdoors performing purposeful work that benefits yourself and others?

If you're interested, call the ranger station nearest you for information.

Gypsy Peak

■ **7,309 Feet**

■ Round-Trip Length: **7 miles** ■ Elevation Gain: **1,749 feet** ■ Hiking Time: **6-7 hours**

Gypsy Peak lies in the roadless Salmo-Priest Wilderness, and though it's the tallest mountain in Eastern Washington, relatively few people know of its status. Thus it's unlikely you'll run into a crowd of hikers swarming the slopes.

The route to Gypsy traverses what is probably the most rugged country in Eastern Washington. Much of the route is at an elevation close to or above 7,000 feet. Though a trail brings you up to the ridge that connects to Gypsy, most of the hike is off-trail along a bare, rocky ridge that is very steep in places. It's a tough hike, but once atop the summit, you'll find the satisfaction of overlooking this untouched land of sculpted rock and placid lakes, of distant streams tumbling downhill was not only worth the effort, leaving it will be a reluctant chore.

The route to Gypsy Peak is the same one used to climb #5 South Fork and #35 Leola Peak. However, because of a yearly road closure, Gypsy Peak cannot be accessed from this trailhead after August 15th.

Getting There

■ From the end of the bridge that spans the Pend Oreille River in Metaline Falls, drive 2.1 miles north on Highway 31.

■ Turn right onto Sullivan Lake Road (County Road 9345) and drive 4.6 miles to Forest Service Road #2212.

■ Turn left onto Road #2212 where a sign points the way to Highline Road and Crowell Ridge. From here, the trailhead's an hour and fifteen minute drive over 18 miles of gravel road.

■ Proceed on Road #2212 until coming to a fork at 3.4 miles. Bear right, taking the Gypsy-Leola Road. At 11.4 miles you'll intersect Crowell Ridge Road #200. Follow the sign and turn left. Though a sign states it's 8 miles to the trailhead at the end of the road, it's actually 6.6 miles.

■ The road passes through a clear-cut on a very steep hillside over the last two miles. Barely driveable by passenger car, there are numerous rough patches and water berms which make driving very slow.

■ Take note of the gate and sign at the intersection of Crowell Ridge Road #200. The last six and a half miles of road is closed to vehicles from August 15th to November 30th of each year to allow an undisturbed habitat for huckleberry-seeking bears.

The Trail

Crowell Ridge Trail #515
Starting Elevation: 5,560 feet
Rating: Huffin' and Puffin'
Info: Sullivan Lake Ranger District
USGS topo map: Gypsy Peak

At the trailhead, you'll see a sign stating it's eight miles to Sullivan Mountain. Take this trail as it climbs through a clear-cut before crossing the Salmo-Priest Wilderness boundary line. The trail continues to climb until after 45 minutes of steady walking you'll reach the top of Crowell Ridge. From here, the trail levels out and turns left (southwest) toward Sullivan Mountain. But at this point you'll turn right, leaving the trail and following the ridge to the north.

You'll be in for some steep climbing in places, but the ridge is open and the view

6,828 feet). Beyond and just to the right of Salmo Mountain, eight miles distant is Snowy Top Mountain (7,572 feet) in Idaho. All mountains lying north from Salmo Mountain are in Canada.

Looking southeast, the rounded, treed summit on the ridge across the valley, about six miles away is Thunder Mountain (#24: 6,560 feet). On the same ridgeline, south of Thunder, the mountain with the two rocky, bald spots and burned summit is Helmer Mountain (#20: 6,734 feet).

Looking just to the right of due south, the pointed peak 17 miles distant is Molybdenite Mountain (#16: 6,784 feet). Just to the right of Molybdenite, the rounded, prominent summit even further in the distance is Calispell Mountain (#14: 6,885 feet).

is great every step of the way. Keep following the ridge and about an hour after leaving the trail, you'll come to a high point which has a magnificent overlook of a hanging valley spread below. At this point you'll be able to see Gypsy Peak for the first time. It is to the north, directly across the valley from you. Down below, Watch Lake lies between yourself and Gypsy.

The route to Gypsy, via the ridgeline that sweeps to your left, is easy to see. Take it, and after another hour of hiking, you'll be standing atop the highest point in Eastern Washington.

From the Summit
Looking directly north, the next-door peak connected by a ridge to Gypsy is South Fork (#5: 7,152 feet). In the valley between yourself and South Fork are two lakes appropriately named Gypsy Lakes.

Looking to the northeast, the lower elevation peak across the valley with the lookout tower is Salmo Mountain. (#15:

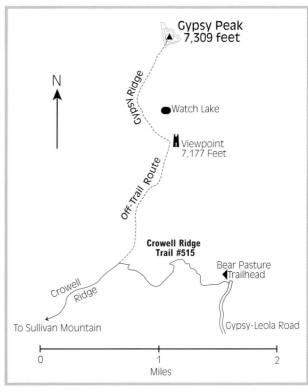

Abercrombie Mountain

7,308 Feet
■ Round-Trip Length: **6.5 miles** ■ Elevation Gain: **3,218 feet** ■ Hiking Time: **4 hours**

If you made a pile of rocks atop this peak, you could transform it into the highest mountain in Eastern Washington since it's number two by only a foot.

Located northeast of Colville, Abercrombie Mountain has a distinctive appearance when seen from a distance. The rocky, southwest-facing slope is decorated with huge, wavy, black bands, dark in some spots, light in others. The black swatches are actually tough lichens eeking out an existence on the mountain's rocks and boulders.

Several miles of hiking trails were constructed on Abercrombie's lower slopes in 1995, and three different trailheads provide access to the mountain. The one described is the shortest, quickest route. It's also the route that brings you within reach of #4 Hooknose Mountain which you may consider climbing as well.

Getting There

■ Heading north on Main Street (Highway 395) through Colville, turn right onto Third St. (Highway 20) and go 1.2 miles to the top of the hill.
■ Turn left onto Aladdin Road. Follow this road for the next 25.4 miles until coming to a three-way intersection.
■ Turn right and drive 7.3 miles, passing Deep Lake until coming to a sign that says "Silver Creek Road." Turn right onto graveled Silver Creek Road. From here it's 9.8 miles to the trailhead.
■ At six-tenths of a mile the road forks. Bear left.
■ At 1.5 miles the road crosses a cattle guard and becomes Forest Service Road 7078.

■ At 1.9 miles the road forks again. To the right is Forest Service Road 070. Don't take it. Go left up the hill and continue until the 6.3 mile mark where you'll turn right onto marked Forest Service Road 300.

The gravel ends here and Road 300 is one of those two-ruts-and-tall-weeds-in-the-middle kind of roads. Though negotiable by low-clearance car, it's slow going as you pass through muddy spots and negotiate several water berms to keep from scraping. You have to endure this for 3 1/2 miles until reaching the trailhead at the end of the road.

The Trail

Abercrombie Mountain Trail No. 117
Starting Elevation: 4,090 feet
Rating: Break a Sweat
Info: Colville Ranger District
USGS topo map: Abercrombie Mountain

The trail begins by switchbacking through a lushly vegetated, old clear-cut until the 1.4 mile mark where it intersects North Fork Silver Creek Trail No. 119. Turn left and from here it's 1.8 miles to the top.

The trail, reconstructed in 1995, soon leaves the dense forest and climbs through the stunted trees of Abercrombie's upper slopes. It makes its way to the ridgeline south of the peak and then follows the open ridge up to the summit.

From the Summit

At the top you'll be rewarded with a spectacular view of the Pend Oreille River valley to the east and beyond it, the Selkirk Mountain Range.

Looking northwest, you can see the ski runs of Red Mountain Ski Resort and just below it, the town of Rossland, British Columbia. Just to the right of Rossland, hidden behind a ridge, is Trail, B.C. which should be marked by the perennial plume of smoke rising from the Cominco Smelter.

Only a couple miles away to the northeast, connected by a ridge, is rocky Hooknose Mountain (#4: 7,210 feet). Looking a little to the right of due south, the knob that rises from the ridge about four miles across the valley is Sherlock Peak (#38: 6,365 feet). Just to the right of Sherlock, the rounded, prominent peak 33

miles away is Calispell Mountain (#14: 6,855 feet). Looking a bit to the left of due south, the rocky mountain about four miles away is Mt. Linton (#45: 6,215 feet).

As you climb the upper slopes, look for the uncommon whitebark pine which grows in profusion on Mt. Abercrombie. This pine, found only at high elevation, has a smooth trunk and needles in clusters of five, unlike the lodgepole pine which also grows here but has needle clusters of two.

If you prefer a full-day hike, Abercrombie can be reached from the North Fork Silver Creek Trailhead. This eight-hour, fifteen-mile hike starts at the end of Forest Service Road #070. To reach it, drive to the intersection 1.9 miles beyond the cattleguard as described above, but instead of turning left, bear right onto Road #070. The trailhead is at the end of the road, 2.3 miles beyond the intersection.

There is yet another trail, #502, which leads west to Abercrombie from the Pend Oreille River valley. For information about it, contact the Sullivan Lake Ranger Station.

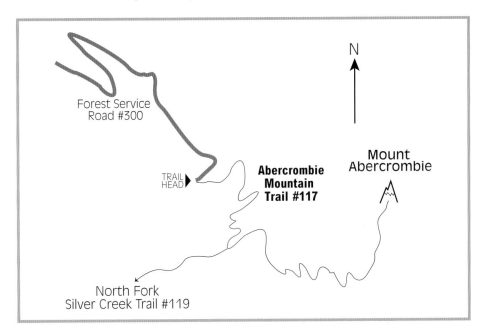

Mount Bonaparte

7,257 Feet

■ Round-Trip Length: **5 miles** ■ Elevation Gain: **2,617 feet** ■ Hiking Time: **3-4 hours**

Despite its height, this prominent mountain in Okanogan County is a relatively short hike. There are four trailheads providing access to Bonaparte. The one described is the Myers Creek trailhead. It's closest to the summit, yet easy to reach.

At the summit you'll find a lookout tower and a hand-hewn log cabin constructed in 1914 that has been listed on the Historic National Register. Though the cabin has been partially restored, most of its timbers are the ones used in the original construction. The skill and craftsmanship of its builders are plainly evident, especially considering the cabin has survived harsh, unforgiving, mountaintop weather for so many years.

The adjacent fire lookout is one of only three on the highest 50 list that are likely to be staffed each summer. Dwindling budgets mean most lookout towers go unmanned during the fire season. Often, lookout towers that are manned depend upon volunteers or workers paid a nominal stipend for their lonely sojourn.

Getting There

■ Drive north on Highway 97 through Tonasket until reaching a sign at the north end of town that points the way to Havillah and Sitzmark Ski Area. Take this road for 17 miles to Havillah where another sign marks the turn-off for West Lost Lake Road.

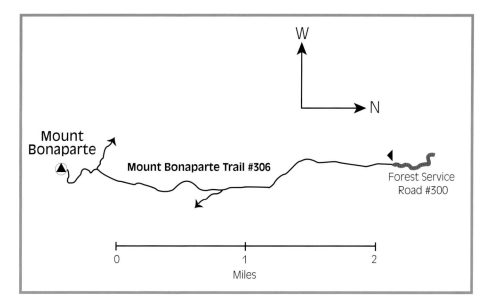

Turn right onto gravelled West Lost Lake Road and drive eight-tenths of a mile to a T-intersection. Turn right onto Forest Service Road #33.

Drive 3.5 miles to marked Forest Service Road #300 where a sign reads, "Bonaparte—2". Turn right.

At 1.4 miles you'll come to the trailhead sign for Bonaparte Trail #306. You can start your hike here, however there's another trailhead for the same trail further up the road. Drive an additional 1.2 miles to find the second trailhead.

The Trail

Mt. Bonaparte Trail #306
Starting Elevation: 4,640 feet
Rating: Break a Swea
Info: Tonasket Ranger District
USGS Maps: Mt. Bonaparte & Havillah

The trail information assumes you'll use the second, higher trailhead. If you start from the lower trailhead, about a mile will be added to your hike each way.

The trail is wide and in good shape all the way to the top. You'll have to put up with some logged landscape at first. But soon you'll be past it and climbing your way through ever-shrinking trees as elevation takes its toll.

You'll pass a couple intersections where trails from other origins feed into the summit trail. The rounded summit makes the hiking easier as you approach the top.

From the Summit

The lookout cabin at the top is a good example of the skill and hard work of Forest Service employees. The cabin's walls are made of logs squared and cut by hand. The unique design has allowed it to survive decades of high winds and severe, mountaintop weather.

Because of the relatively flat summit, you'll have to climb the stairs of the lookout tower to give yourself a good view of the surrounding valleys.

Looking to the southwest, Tonasket is easy to see far below. The Okanogan River valley lies between yourself and the snow-capped peaks of the Cascades to the west. The prominent, rounded mountain lying due south 30 miles away is Moses Mountain (#18: 6,774 feet). The Kettle Range is the line of mountains that lie 30-35 miles to the east.

Hooknose Mountain

7,210 Feet

■ Round-Trip Length: **10-11 miles** ■ Elevation Gain: **3,120 feet** ■ Hiking Time: **6-7 hours**

This rocky, rugged mountain northeast of Colville is a good place to go if you need a fix of mountain scenery and uncrowded wilderness. Not many people hike this mountain due to its remote location and the lack of a summit trail. However, it can still be climbed as a day hike, and the off-trail portion is easy going through mostly open, subalpine landscape.

Mt. Hooknose is unique in that its steep east side facing the Pend Oreille River valley gives the effect of being perched almost directly above the valley. Since the elevation difference between the summit and the valley below is more than 5,000 feet, you get a bird's-eye perspective unlike any other mountain view in Eastern Washington. This is one mountaintop where you'll want to linger and savor the rich views.

Getting There

■ Since hiking to Hooknose Mountain involves using the Mt. Abercrombie Trail, the directions for the two mountains are the same. From Highway 395 in Colville, turn east onto Third Street (Highway 20) and go 1.2 miles to the top of the hill.

■ Turn left onto Aladdin Road and drive 25.4 miles until coming to a Y-intersection.

■ Bear right and drive 7.3 miles, going past Deep Lake until reaching graveled Silver Creek Road. Turn right. From here it's 9.8 miles to the trailhead.

■ At six-tenths of a mile the road forks. Bear left.

■ At 1.5 miles you'll cross a cattle guard and the road becomes Forest Service Road 7078.

■ At 1.9 miles the road forks again. Take the unmarked road to the left that heads uphill.

■ At 6.3 miles watch for a right turn that is marked Forest Service Road No. 300. Take this rough road that is a challenge, but negotiable for passenger cars. Drive all the way to the trailhead at the end of the road.

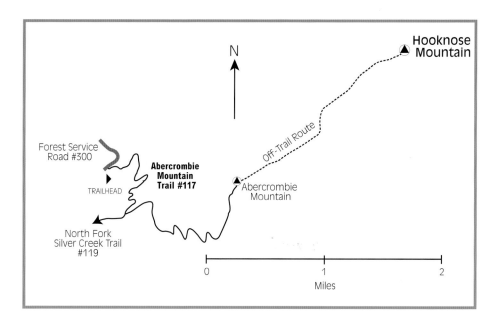

The Trail

Abercrombie Mountain Trail No. 117
Starting Elevation: 4,090 feet
Rating: Huffin' & Puffin'
Info: Colville Ranger Dist
USGS topo map: Abercrombie Mountain

Climbing Hooknose Mountain is a 2 for 1 package since you'll climb #2 Abercrombie Mountain in the process. From the trailhead, follow Trail No. 117 as it switchbacks through an old clear-cut. At 1.4 miles the trail intersects the North Fork Silver Creek Trail. Go left and walk 1.8 miles to the top of Abercrombie.

From the top of Abercrombie, Hooknose Mountain can easily be seen at the end of the ridgeline that runs to the northeast. Simply follow this ridgeline. Descending Abercrombie's peak is the steepest section, but past it the walking is fairly easy. You may find an old trail that appears intermittently along the ridgeline. It's approximately two miles from Abercrombie to the summit of Hooknose.

From the Summit

Looking southeast from the top of Hooknose, you can see the concrete towers of the old cement factory that mark the town of Metaline Falls. Looking in the distance nearly due south, the Pend Oreille River is visible.

Looking northward, the hundreds of jagged peaks that spread from horizon to horizon make it seem British Columbia is nothing but uninhabitable, mountainous terrain.

If you gaze due east, thirteen miles across the Pend Oreille River valley, you can see Gypsy Peak (#1: 7,309 feet), the highest point of several peaks along Gypsy Ridge.

Turning your gaze due south, you can see rocky Mt. Linton (#45: 6,215 feet) five miles away.

Looking down Hooknose's steep north side, you'll see circular Hooknose Lake way below. Don't scramble down with your fishing pole though—it has no fish.

South Fork 5

7,152 Feet
■ Round-Trip Length: **10 miles** ■ Elevation Gain: **1,592 feet** ■ Hiking Time: **9-10 hours**

This peak in the Salmo-Priest Wilderness will be a test for your legs and ankles. It is a long, up and down, ridge-walking, boulder-hopping climb. In reaching South Fork, you'll bag the summit of #1 Gypsy Peak as well as spend most of the day at or above 7,000 feet elevation.

This hike is a fun, exploratory climb along an open ridge that gives unobstructed views along the entire route. It's mostly off-trail, thus you'll likely encounter few if any people as you make your way across this remote, lightly traveled country.

Though reachable on a day hike, it's a long one, and reaching the trailhead can take a few hours depending on where you live. From Sullivan Lake, the trailhead is more than an hour's drive away over a narrow, gravel road. You may want to camp at Sullivan Lake to get an early morning start.

Keep in mind that the road to the trailhead is closed every summer on August 15th.

Getting There
■ From the end of the bridge spanning the Pend Oreille River in Metaline Falls, drive 2.1 miles north on Highway 31. Turn right onto Sullivan Lake Road (County Road #9345).
■ Drive 4.6 miles to graveled Forest Service Road #2212 which is marked by a sign that points the way to Highline Road and Crowell Ridge.
■ Turn left and drive 3.4 miles until reaching a fork. To the left is the Sullivan Mountain Lookout Tower Road. Bear right onto Gypsy-Leola Road.
■ At 11.4 miles you'll intersect Road

#200. Follow the sign and turn left. A mileage sign at this point says it's 8 miles to the trailhead at the end of the road, but it's actually 6.6 miles. At this point you'll also pass the gate that closes the road on August 15th.
■ The road is negotiable by passenger car, but the last two miles passes through a clear-cut on a very steep hillside. The road here is narrow, bumpy, and contains numerous water berms, making driving very slow.

The Trail
Crowell Ridge Trail #515
Starting Elevation: 5,560 feet
Rating: Major Workout
Info: Sullivan Lake Ranger District
USGS topo map: Gypsy Peak

Take Crowell Ridge Trail as it ascends through a clear-cut before crossing the boundary line into the Salmo-Priest Wilderness. Close to 45 minutes of steady uphill walking will bring you to the top of Crowell Ridge. The trail levels out here and turns left (southwest) for Sullivan Mountain. Instead, turn right and leave the trail.

Follow the ridge as it rises and falls until coming to a high point after about an hour of off-trail walking. You will see a lake nestled in a hanging valley below you. The peak directly across the valley from you is Gypsy Mountain. Continue following the ridge to the left until arriving after another hour of hiking at the summit of Gypsy. From there you'll get a glimpse of South Fork for the first time. It is due north, on the other side of yet another hanging valley. The two Gypsy Lakes lie in

From the Summit

Looking to the northeast, the mountain across the valley with the lookout tower is Salmo Mountain (#15: 6,828 feet). Beyond Salmo, the prominent, three-pronged mountain eight miles distant is Snowy Top Mountain (7,572 feet) in Idaho.

If you look southwest, about seven miles away, the peak at the end of Crowell Ridge with its lookout tower barely visible is Sullivan Mountain (#29: 6,483 feet).

Looking just left of Gypsy Peak, you'll see a rounded mountain about eight miles away with a burned summit and two patches of bare rock on its north-facing slope. This is Helmer Mountain (#20: 6,734 feet).

Looking roughly 15 miles to the north-east, you may be surprised to see a highway cut into the high slopes of the Selkirk Mountains. It is Kootenai Pass on Highway 3 in British Columbia. It's the highest mountain pass in Canada that's open year-round.

Finally, gazing due west, you can see a portion of the Pend Oreille River where it's backed up behind Boundary Dam.

the valley between yourself and South Fork. The way to South Fork is easy to see. Continue following the ridge as it sweeps in a semi-circle to the summit. It's about a 75-minute hike from Gypsy.

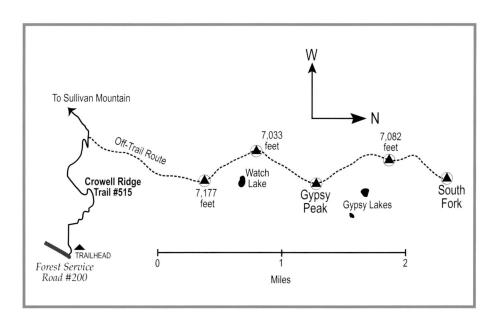

Copper Butte

7,140 Feet

■ Round-Trip Length: **6 miles** ■ Elevation Gain: **1,640 feet** ■ Hiking Time: **3 hours**

The highest point in both Ferry County and the Kettle Range, part of the route to Copper Butte follows an old stage coach road built in the 1890s and maintained today as a hiking trail. With the trailhead located close by, the hike to the summit is relatively short. However the trail is quite steep over the last half of the route.

A fire consumed nearly 11,000 acres of forest surrounding Copper Butte in 1994. Much of the trail now passes through burned, blackened woods. Despite this, it's still a hike that packs plenty of scenic punch.

The summit of Copper Butte escaped the devastation of the blaze. Stunted sub-alpine firs dominate the flat, expansive mountaintop, but there's still plenty of open space that allows viewing in all directions.

Getting There

■ From Kettle Falls, drive west on Highway 395 across the Columbia River and turn left onto Highway 20 toward Sherman Pass.

■ Drive 18.4 miles to Albion Hill Road #2030.

■ Turn right and follow this well-maintained gravel road for 7.3 miles to the trailhead sign and parking lot.

The Trail

Old Stage Road Trail #75 and Kettle Crest Trail #13

Starting Elevation: 5,500 feet

Rating: Break a Sweat

Info: Colville Ranger District

USGS topo map: Copper Butte

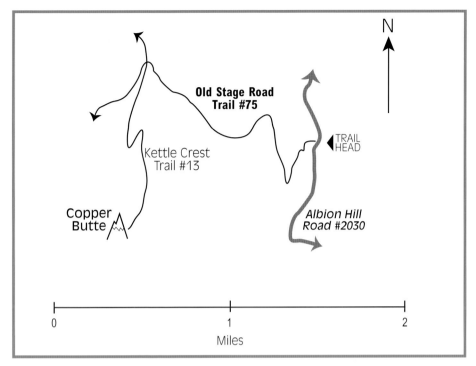

A lone whitetail deer passes through a lush meadow in the Kettle Range.

Leaving the trailhead, the Old Stage Road, constructed in 1892, ascends gently through the thickly-treed lower slopes of Copper Butte. The roadway is still in good enough shape for use by stagecoach traffic, should the need arise again someday.

Soon the road enters the burn area before reaching the saddle between Copper Butte and Midnight Mountain, the peak to the north. From here, the stage road descends down the other side. Follow it down for just a few yards and you'll see the Kettle Crest trail heading upward on the left. Turn off and take it as it climbs the back (west) side of Copper Butte. This section is more demanding than the stage road as it switchbacks through burned timber until reaching the top.

From the Summit

At the top you'll find a series of rock cairns and the remains of an old lookout tower. The next-door peak to the north is Midnight Mountain (#21: 6,660 feet). In the opposite direction to the south is Scar Mountain (#8: 7,046 feet). Both are reachable from Copper Butte if you have the will and the energy.

A great view of the Curlew Lake valley to the west can be had and further in the distance, if it is clear, the North Cascades. What looks like a lake that can be seen looking this way is the tailings pond of the Echo Bay Gold Mine near Republic.

Snow Peak

7,103 Feet
■ Round-Trip Length: **9 miles** ■ Elevation Gain: **1,528 feet** ■ Hiking Time: **6 hours**
(Northwest Forest Pass required)

Snow Peak, the second highest mountain in the Kettle Range, lies just a couple miles south of Highway 20 at Sherman Pass. It's a steep, rocky climb that will take you through the huge White Mountain Burn of 1988.

The Kettle Crest Trail brings you close to Snow Peak, but there's no path leading to the summit, so you'll have to strike off on your own from the trail. There are some odd rock formations to see as you make your way to the top, scrambling and climbing over boulders and rock fields. Though the route is demanding, you'll be richly rewarded with a stunning view. The summit is open, allowing long-distance views in every direction, and the rocky ridgeline that extends south from the peak also beckons exploration.

Getting There

■ Snow Peak is accessed by the Kettle Crest Trail at the top of Sherman Pass. From Kettle Falls, drive west on Highway 395 across the Columbia River and turn left onto Highway 20.

■ Drive 22.6 miles to the top of the pass. Turn right onto the marked dirt road that leads to the trailhead just off the highway.

The Trail

Kettle Crest South Trail No. 13
Starting Elevation: 5,575 feet
Rating: Huffin' & Puffin'
Info: Colville Ranger District
USGS topo map: Sherman Peak

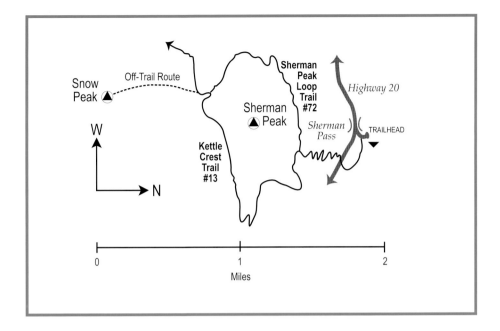

From the top of Sherman Pass, take South Kettle Crest Trail No. 13. The trail skirts a gully before crossing the highway and switchbacking up a heavily forested slope.

About a half hour into the hike you'll come to a fork. The trail to the right goes around Sherman Peak via the west side. The trail to the left crosses a creek and goes around Sherman via the east side. They join together again on the other side so it doesn't matter which one you take. However the trail to the right is about a half mile shorter.

At the point where the trails rejoin on the other (south) side of Sherman Peak, you're at the saddle between Sherman Peak and Snow Peak, to the south. Leave the trail and ascend Snow Peak along the ridgeline on its north side. The lower slopes are steepest as you climb through boulder fields and occasional timber stands. But the going gets easier when you reach the shoulder about half way up. It's here you'll find large, flat slabs of rock surrounding fissure-like trenches.

The rest of the way up passes through stunted stands of Englemann spruce and subalpine fir that escaped the fire. It takes about an hour of steady climbing to reach the top after leaving the trail.

From the Summit

Looking to the north from where you came, the summit of neighboring Sherman Peak (#10: 7,011 feet) is about a mile away. Looking roughly southwest, the pointy-peaked mountain next door about two miles away is Bald Mountain (#11: 6,940 ft).

Looking just left of due south, the broad and rocky summit of White Mountain (#12: 6,921 feet) is visible four miles distant. The lower elevation mountain that lies between yourself and White Mountain is Barnaby Buttes (#27: 6,534 feet).

Looking west, there are two rounded, prominent peaks in the far distance. One is Mt. Bonaparte in Okanogan County (#3: 7,257 feet) to the northwest, 35 miles away. And the other, a little south of due east, 30 miles distant is Moses Mountain (#18: 6,774 feet) on the Colville Indian Reservation.

Scar Mountain

7,046 Feet

■ Round-Trip Length: **10 miles** ■ Elevation Gain: **2,046 feet** ■ Hiking Time: **6 hours**

Scar Mountain, the third highest peak in the Kettle Range, lies sandwiched between two 7,000-footers, Wapaloosie Mountain and Copper Butte. If you get an early start, it's possible to climb all three mountains in one day.

Though there is no trail leading to the summit, you can approach it by taking the Kettle Crest Trail. A 3/4-mile off-trail hike is required to reach the summit, but the way up is through mostly open landscape that's not too steep.

The Kettle Range has more peaks in the Top 50 list than any other range in Eastern Washington. It is also very accessible, with several peaks lying just a few miles off a major highway. The greatest thing though is the trails are well-marked and maintained, yet it gets very light use. This area is truly a hiker's paradise.

Getting There

■ From Kettle Falls, head west on Highway 395 and turn left onto Highway 20 after crossing the Columbia River.

■ Drive 18.4 miles to Albion Hill Road #2030. Turn right and follow this graveled road for 3.3 miles until arriving at the signed Wapaloosie Trailhead on the left.

The Trail

Wapaloosie Trail #15 and Kettle Crest Trail North #13.

Starting Elevation: 5,000 feet

Rating: Huffin' and Puffin'

Info: Colville Ranger District

USGS topo map: Copper Butte

From the trailhead, take Wapaloosie Trail up the east slope of Wapaloosie Mountain

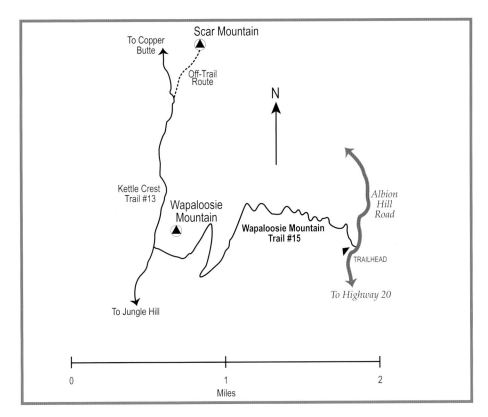

for two and a 1/2 miles until it intersects Kettle Crest Trail #13. Turn right onto the Kettle Crest Trail. If desired, you can take a 10-minute side trip to top Wapaloosie since the summit is close by. Otherwise, follow the Kettle Crest Trail as it descends the west side of Wapaloosie.

The mountain to the north, next to Wapaloosie is Scar Mountain. The trail will soon drop into the saddle between Wapaloosie and Scar Mountain. The saddle is fairly deep, and at the low point, you'll see a slope of boulders to your right. It's about a quarter mile past this point where you'll leave the trail. As you head up the south slope of Scar, the trail will soon make four switchbacks in quick succession. On the fourth and last switchback, turn off the trail and head uphill. This is the most moderately sloped and open route to the top. It's about a half hour climb to the summit.

From the Summit

Though the summit is heavily timbered with stunted subalpine fir, lodgepole, and whitebark pine, there are open areas that allow views in most directions. The neighboring mountain to the south, the direction from which you came, is Wapaloosie Mountain. (#9: 7,018 ft). The next-door peak to the north is Copper Butte (#6: 7,140 feet).

Looking due east, the lower-elevation mountain across the valley with the summit barely two miles away is King Mountain (#22: 6,634 feet).

If you look a little to the left of northwest, the rounded, prominent peak 30 miles distant is Mt. Bonaparte (#3: 7,257 feet) in Okanogan County. If the day is clear, even further to the west you can see the snowy, jagged peaks of the North Cascades.

Wapaloosie Mountain

7,018 Feet

Round-Trip Length: **5.6 miles** ■ Elevation Gain: **2,018 feet** ■ Hiking Time: **3 hours**

Wapaloosie Mountain, with its bare upper slopes and rounded summit, is a pleasant, scenic hike that allows a constant bird's-eye view of the surrounding forests. This mountain is also one of five 7,000-footers in the Kettle Range, the largest concentration of 7,000-foot peaks in Eastern Washington.

Though the Wapaloosie trail doesn't reach the summit, it comes close enough to leave only a short, off-trail jaunt to the top. This is also a short hike—trailhead to mountaintop is only 2.8 miles. The first part of the trail passes through thick timber, but much of the upper half of the trail passes through an expansive, grassy slope which provides excellent views.

Getting There

■ From Kettle Falls, head west on Highway 395 across the Columbia River and turn left onto Highway 20 after crossing the bridge.

■ Drive 18.4 miles to marked Albion Hill Road #2030. Turn right and follow this graveled road for 3.3 miles until arriving at the signed trailhead on the left.

The Trail

Wapaloosie Trail #15
Starting Elevation: 5,000 feet
Rating: Break a Sweat
Info: Colville Ranger District
USGS topo map: Copper Butte

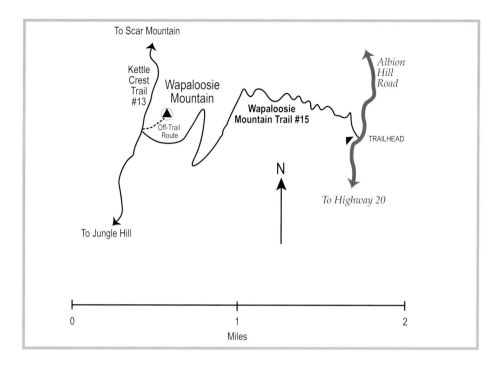

A curious coyote pup sits outside his den on Bald Mountain.

Wapaloosie Mountain Trail #15 begins climbing the east slope of Wapaloosie through a thick forest of lodgepole pine. After a mile or so, you'll leave the woods and switchback your way through the open upper slopes. Though the slope is very steep, the trail maintains a moderate grade that's not so hard to handle. When you reach the top of the ridge where the

trail intersects Kettle Crest Trail #13, the summit of Wapaloosie is to your right, barely a quarter mile away. From here the Kettle Crest Trail will soon begin descending Wapaloosie on its back (west) side. Leave the trail and head up the open, gentle slope. In less than ten minutes you'll be standing on the summit.

From the Summit

The view from Wapaloosie allows you to see all the major peaks of the Kettle Crest, and on a clear day, the North Cascades.

Looking eastward across the valley, the mountain that has replanted trees growing in rows about three miles away is King Mountain (#22: 6,634 feet). The next-door mountain to the north is Scar Mountain. (#8: 7,046 feet). If you have time, Scar is easily reached from Wapaloosie.

The next mountain beyond Scar, a little less than three miles away, is Copper Butte. (#6: 7,140 feet) the highest mountain in the Kettle Range.

Sherman Peak 10

7,011 Feet
■ Round-Trip Length: **6 miles** ■ Elevation Gain: **1,433 feet** ■ Hiking Time: **4 hours**
(Northwest Forest Pass required)

Rising steeply on the south side of Highway 20 at Sherman Pass, the pointed, bare rocky top, and burned slopes make Sherman Peak easy to identify. On many road maps its elevation is listed as 6,998 feet But according to U.S. Geological Survey maps, Sherman Peak is in the 7,000-foot club.

In 1988, the lightning-caused White Mountain Fire engulfed Sherman Peak and several other nearby peaks. Over 20,000 acres were burned when the fire broke out over a hot, windy Labor Day weekend.

Because of its proximity to Highway 20, Sherman Peak is a moderate, though steep day hike. The Kettle Crest Trail brings hikers close to the summit, but the last half mile is off-trail through open woodlands and boulder fields. If a full day of hiking is desired, climb both Sherman and #7 Snow Peak, the neighboring mountain to the south.

Getting There

■ From Kettle Falls, drive westward on Highway 395 across the Columbia River and turn left onto Highway 20.

■ Drive 22.6 miles to the top of Sherman Pass on Highway 20. A sign at the top marks the turnoff for the Kettle Crest Trailhead.

The Trail

Kettle Crest Trail South No. 13
Starting Elevation: 5,575 feet
Rating: Break a Sweat
Info: Colville Ranger District
USGS topo map: Sherman Peak

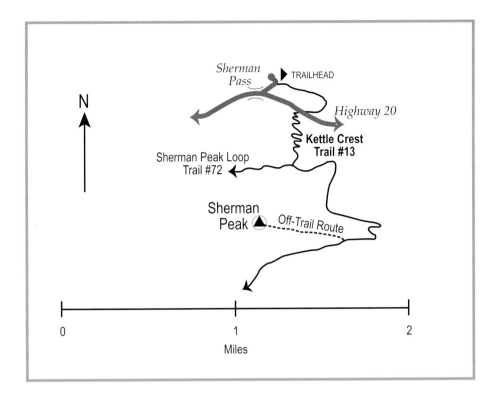

From the trailhead, ignore the North Kettle Crest Trailhead and take the South Kettle Crest Trail as it meanders around a gully before crossing the highway. About a half hour into the hike, the trail forks. The two trails come back together on the other side of Sherman. But for this hike, you'll want to bear left, taking the wooden bridge across the stream.

The trail switchbacks through heavily forested slopes until reaching the burned area. From this point on there's little protection from the sun. A hat or sunscreen is a good idea.

The trail climbs continuously until leveling out when it reaches a plateau of sorts on Sherman's east side. A few minutes of flat walking on this plateau will lead you to the last slope that leads to Sherman's summit. As the trail abuts the slope leading upward, you can eyeball the best spot to leave the trail and head up. The going is fairly easy through a burned area of grasses and rock outcroppings. After leaving the trail, it shouldn't take but 20 to 30 minutes to reach the top. About 100 yards from the top, you'll have to scramble over a boulder field to reach the summit.

From the Summit

From Sherman Peak, an excellent view of the entire Kettle Range is possible. Immediately to the north on the other side of the highway is Columbia Mountain (#17: 6,782 feet). Looking the opposite direction to the south, the peak next door is Snow Peak (#7: 7,103 feet). Ambitious hikers can conquer it after descending Sherman.

Continuing to look roughly south, the pointed summit beyond Snow Peak, three miles away is Bald Mountain (#11: 6,940 feet). And visible just to the left of Snow's summit, five miles distant is White Mountain (#12: 6,921 feet).

Bald Mountain

6,940 Feet

Round-Trip Length: **14 miles** ▪ Elevation Gain: **1,365 feet** ▪ Hiking Time: **10 hours**
(Northwest Forest Pass required)

This soaring peak in the Kettle Range will give you an excellent, unencumbered view, but you'll have to work for it. It's a daylong, rollercoaster of a hike that requires a vertical climb several hundred feet greater than the difference between the trailhead elevation and the summit's.

Bald Mountain likely earned its name for its bare, lifeless summit. From a distance, it's obviously rocky and unvegetated. But the peak is actually a mass of huge, lichen-encrusted boulders, piled up as if a giant had placed them in a symmetrical heap.

If it's a clear day, take note of the plain but stark contrast when you reach the summit. The blue sky above and the boulders that surround you are such simple things that occupy our everyday world, but sitting there, it's an impressive contrast that awes and inspires.

Getting There

▪ From Kettle Falls, drive west on Highway 395 across the Columbia River and turn left onto Highway 20 after crossing the bridge.
▪ Drive 22.6 miles to the top of Sherman Pass. Turn right at the sign pointing the way to the Kettle Crest Trailhead just off the highway.

The Trail

Kettle Crest Trail #13 and Edds
   Mountain Trail #3
Rating: Major Workout
Info: Colville Ranger District
Starting Elevation: 5,575 feet
USGS topo map: Edds Mountain &
   Sherman Peak.

This hike uses the same trail as #7 Snow Peak and #10 Sherman Peak. From the trailhead, take the South Kettle Crest Trail #13. The trail skirts a gully before crossing the highway and ascending through a thick forest. After about a half hour, you'll come to a fork in the trail. Either one can be taken as the two trails come back together on the other side of Sherman Peak, but the trail to the right is about a half mile shorter.

You'll enter the White Mountain burn as you pass by Sherman Peak and when you reach the junction where the trails re-join, you'll be at the saddle of Sherman Peak to the north, and Snow Peak to the south. From here on, the trail cuts across the west-facing slope of Snow Peak. Along most of this section, the pointed summit of Bald Mountain will be plainly visible ahead of you.

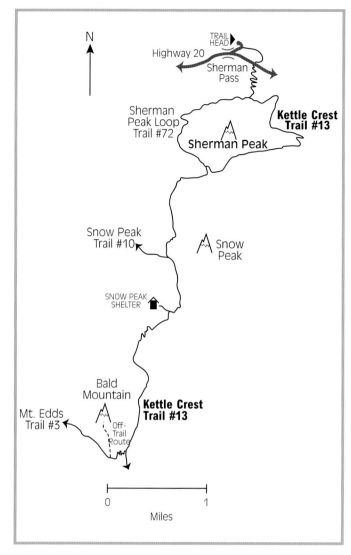

ascend steeply for 20 minutes until reaching a shoulder of sorts on Bald Mountain's south-facing slope. When the trail levels out on the shoulder, it becomes even harder to follow. The trail heads east to Edds Mountain however, so you'll have to leave it anyway and head upslope. The walking is easy through the open, grassy slope. In about a half hour you should be standing at the summit.

From the Summit

Looking at the valley to the northwest you can just see the southern end of Curlew Lake about 15 miles away.

Looking northward in the direction from which you came, Snow Peak (#7: 7,103 feet) is the neighboring mountain and beyond it is Sherman Peak (#10: 7,011 feet). Turning your gaze the opposite direction, White Mountain (#12: 6,921 feet) is the tall peak toward the southeast, roughly four miles away. The lower-elevation mountain between yourself and White Mountain is Barnaby Buttes (#26: 6,534 feet)

Looking due west, the broad peak topped by a forest of gray snags is Edds Mountain (#25: 6,550 feet), two miles away.

As you near Bald Mountain, the trail will begin descending. In short order you'll find yourself on Bald's east slope, far below the summit, still descending and being taken past the peak. Don't worry. The trail soon intersects with Edds Mountain Trail #3 on the right. You may find a weathered sign laying on the ground here. However, since the trail is no longer maintained, it and the sign may be hard to spot. Watch for a stream that crosses the trail near the intersection.

Once on Edds Mountain Trail, you'll

White Mountain

6,921 Feet

■ Round-Trip Length: **6 miles** ■ Elevation Gain: **1,761 feet** ■ Hiking Time: **4 hours**

White Mountain is the southernmost peak in the Kettle Crest Trail system, and easily reached from the trailhead at the southern terminus. Though a lofty mountain, the proximity of the trailhead makes this a moderate hike compared to other mountains on the list.

This peak is the namesake of the 20,000-acre White Mountain Fire of 1988. Though several portions of the trail pass through burned areas, there are still numerous treed sections that escaped the blaze. However the high elevation and southern aspect result in a naturally open landscape that gives fabulous views for much of the hike.

Getting There

■ From Kettle Falls, drive west on Highway 395 across the Columbia River. Turn left onto Highway 20 after crossing the river.

■ Drive 10.4 miles and turn left onto signed South Fork Sherman Creek Road #2020. From here it's 14.7 miles of well-maintained gravel road to the trailhead.

■ At mile 6.5, the road forks. Bear left onto Barnaby Creek Rd. #2014.

■ Stay on Barnaby Creek Road until milepoint 10.4 where the road forks again. Follow the sign, turning right onto Road #250. Drive to the end of the maintained road at mile 14.7 where you'll find the trailhead sign and parking lot.

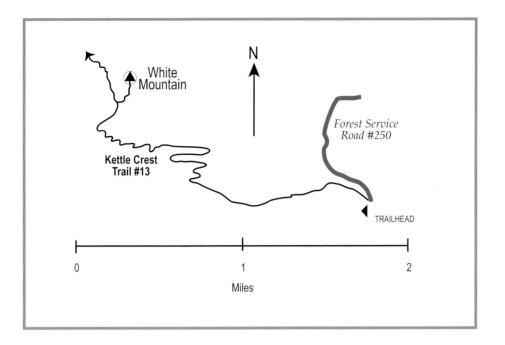

The Trail

Kettle Crest Trail #13
Starting Elevation: 5,160 feet
Rating: Break a Sweat
Info: Colville Ranger District
USGS topo map: Sherman Peak

The trail begins by climbing White Mountain's south-facing slope. What appears to be the summit, which you can see from the trailhead, is actually a shoulder which you'll be able to look down upon later in the hike.

The ascent is generally moderate with only a few short, steep sections. As you approach the top, the trail begins to head down the other side without going to the highest point on the mountain. However, shortly after the trail begins to descend, you'll come to a spur trail on the right in the middle of a meadow. This trail looks more like a small gully caused by run-off. Take it anyhow, and on the first tree you come to there's a weathered sign attached that says "trail". The path is a little rough, but in less than 10 minutes, you'll arrive at the top.

From the Summit

The top is rocky and sparsely treed with clumps of subalpine fir. Remains of an old lookout tower are visible. Looking to the east and southeast, long stretches of the Columbia River are easily visible. Looking almost due west, the tall, rounded, prominent mountain thirty miles distant is Moses Mountain (#18: 6,774 feet,) on the Colville Indian Reservation.

If you make your way through a stand of burned trees at the north end of the sum-mit, you can see pointed, rocky Bald Mountain. (#11: 6,940 feet) about four miles to the northwest. The lower-elevation mountain with two rounded humps and open grassland between yourself and Bald Mountain is Barnaby Buttes (#27: 6,534 feet).

To the right of Bald, across the valley is Snow Peak (#7: 7,103 feet). Behind Snow Peak, the rocky, rounded summit six miles distant is Sherman Peak (#10: 7,011 feet).

Crowell Ridge

6,885 Feet
■ Round-Trip Length: **8 miles** ■ Elevation Gain: **1,325 feet** ■ Hiking Time: **6 hours**

Located in the Salmo-Priest Wilderness, Crowell Ridge is a remote, backcountry hike through a grassy, open, subalpine landscape. Most of the hike is above 6,500 feet elevation, and it's late June or early July before the trail is snow-free.

Crowell Ridge Trail No. 515 runs the length of the ridge from the Bear Pasture Trailhead to Sullivan Mountain. However, the high point of Crowell is about midway between Sullivan Mountain and the trailhead, and requires a short off-trail walk.

Access to the trailhead at Bear Pasture is restricted after August 15th each year. The trail itself is never closed, but the road to the trailhead is gated for wildlife considerations. If desired, you can still reach Crowell Ridge after August 15th by beginning your hike from Sullivan Mountain.

Getting There
■ From the end of the bridge crossing the Pend Oreille River in Metaline Falls, drive 2.1 miles north on Highway 31 to Sullivan Lake Road.
■ Turn right and drive 4.6 miles to Forest Service Road #2212, marked by a sign reading "Highline Road" and "Crowell Ridge." Turn left, and from here, the trailhead is about an hour and fifteen minutes of driving over 18 miles of gravel road.
■ At 3.4 miles, the road forks. To the left is the Sullivan Mountain Lookout Tower Road. Bear right, taking Gypsy-Leola Road.
■ At 11.4 miles, you'll come to a T-intersection marked by a sign reading, "End of Road 8 miles". Follow the sign and turn left, driving to Bear Pasture Trailhead at the end of the road which is actually 6.6 miles distant.

■ The entire route is passable by low-clearance vehicle. However, the road passes through a clear-cut on a very steep hillside over the last two miles, and you'll have to drive slowly to negotiate the numerous bumps and water berms.

The Trail
Crowell Ridge Trail #515
Starting Elevation: 5,560 feet
Rating: Break a Sweat
Info: Sullivan Lake Ranger District
USGS topo map: Gypsy Peak

At the trailhead, you'll find a trailhead register and a sign stating that it's eight miles to Sullivan Mountain. You'll cover about half that distance to reach the high point of Crowell Ridge.

The trail passes through an old clear-cut before crossing the boundary line into the Salmo-Priest Wilderness. After 45 minutes of moderate uphill climbing, the trail reaches the top of Crowell Ridge and turns to the southwest.

You'll see a series of knobs and rises ahead of you, however, the trail skirts most of the knobs without topping them. The fourth knob you come to, which you

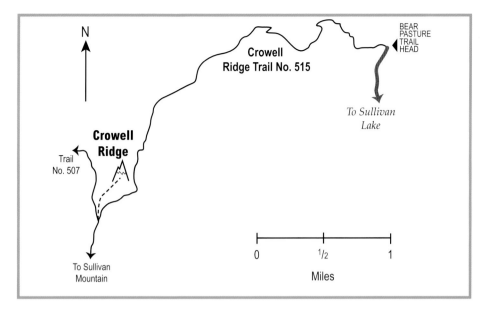

should be able to recognize as the highest, is your destination. You should also see the remains of an old lookout cabin as you approach the peak.

The trail however passes the summit, staying well below it until coming to a junction marked by two weathered signs. Here, Trail 507 connects with Crowell Ridge Trail. Though you've walked past Crowell's summit, this is the high point of the trail and the route to the top is easiest from here. Turn back in the direction from which you came and head up. In 10 to15 minutes you'll be at the top.

From the Summit

At the top you'll find an old, collapsed cabin used by fire lookouts decades ago. Looking due east across the valley, the next-door mountain about two miles distant is Prouty Peak (#41: 6,263 ft). On the next ridge beyond Prouty Peak, the rounded knob, 4-5 miles away is Thunder Mountain (#24: 6,560 feet). Following the ridge to the right from Thunder, the next mountain, with a burned summit and a pair of bald, rocky spots on its north face, is Helmer Mountain (#20: 6,734 feet).

All the rocky peaks eastward in the far distance are the Selkirk Mountains of north Idaho.

If you look roughly north and follow the ridge you stand on, three prominent high points rise in the distance. The highest of these is Gypsy Peak (#1: 7,309 feet) about 5 miles away.

Looking southwest, Sullivan Mountain (#29: 6,483 feet) is easily visible, marked by the lookout tower. If you look just to the right of due south, the mountain across the valley, 5-6 miles away, is Hall Mountain (#39: 6,323 feet). Just to the left of Hall's summit, 12-13 miles distant, you'll see the pointed peak of Molybdenite Mountain (#16: 6,784 feet). And to the right of Molybdenite, even further in the distance, 25 or so miles away, the rounded, prominent peak is Calispell Mountain (#14: 6,855 feet).

If you look nearly due west across the Pend Oreille River valley, thirteen miles away you can see Abercrombie Mountain (#2: 7,308 feet) which is marked by clear-cuts on its lower slopes. Two miles to the right of Abercrombie, connected by a ridge, is Hooknose Mountain (#4: 7,210 ft).

The Crowell Ridge trail terminates at #29 Sullivan Mountain, where it is accessed by the Sullivan Mountain lookout road.

Calispell Peak

6,855 Feet
■ Round-Trip Length: **10 miles** ■ Elevation Gain: **2,450 feet** ■ Hiking Time: **6 hours**

For the hiker who spends time in the high country of Eastern Washington, Calispell Peak soon becomes a familiar sight. Located northeast of Chewelah, Calispell stands alone, rising well above its lower-elevation neighbors. This high visibility allows it to be easily seen and identified from miles away.

Because of its prominence and easy access, Calispell Peak is a popular play area and possibly the most scaled mountain of the highest 50 in Eastern Washington. A rough and rutted road leads to the summit, and the lower slopes are crossed by a maze of logging roads. The buzz of off-road vehicles can be heard in summer and fall, and when the snow comes, the snowmobilers take over, turning the mountain into a winter playland.

Because of past heavy logging, as well as the heavy use, Calispell isn't such a pretty hike, nor a good place for quiet solitude. But it is one of the higher mountains in Eastern Washington, and it's a great vista at the top.

Getting There
■ From Cusick, drive 3.9 miles north on State Highway 20. Follow the sign that points the way to the USAF Survival School by turning left onto graveled Tacoma Creek Road (Also Pend Oreille County Rd. #2389).

■ Drive past the survival school to the 6.5 mile marker and turn left onto marked Forest Service Road #629. From here, it's about 11 miles to the summit of Calispell Peak.

■ A short distance beyond the intersection, a marker shows that Forest Service Road 629 changes to Road 630. At about 3.8 miles the road forks. Follow the sign and bear left.

■ Not far past the fork, the road becomes increasingly rough. Soon you'll need a tough, four-wheel-drive vehicle to continue, or you may even have your way blocked by downed trees. If you're driving a low-clearance passenger car, you'll be able to negotiate the first five or six miles before road conditions stop you, leaving a hike of about equal distance to the summit.

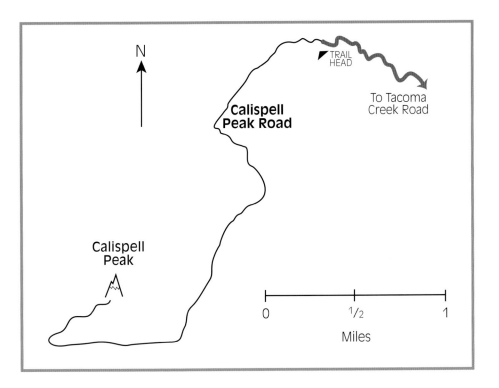

The Trail

Forest Service Road #630
Starting Elevation: 4,400 feet
Rating: Break a Sweat
Info: Colville Ranger District
USGS topo map: Calispell Peak

Assuming you park your car halfway up the summit road, you'll have about a 10 to 11 mile day hike, which isn't as tough as it seems since the roadway ascends moderately and the walking is easy.

For the first 3 or 4 miles you'll pass stands of mostly small-diameter lodgepole and fir before coming to the open upper slopes. There are occasional intersections at which you'll always take the ascending road straight ahead. The road switchbacks a half mile prior to delivering you at the rounded, open summit.

From the Summit

At the top you'll be able to see how this area has been extensively logged. You'll also see that there are several routes to the summit since logging roads approach the peak from nearly every direction.

Looking just right of due south, the ski runs of 49 Degrees North Ski Area on Chewelah Mountain are easily visible about 10 miles away. If you look to the southeast, the twin humps of Mt. Spokane and Mt. Kit Carson can be seen, 25 or so miles away.

To the east, a long stretch of the Pend Oreille River is visible, and beyond it, the many peaks of the Selkirk Range in Idaho. Looking due north, 33 miles distant, a pair of pointed peaks sitting close to one another, connected by a ridge, are Mt. Hooknose (#4: 7,210 feet) to the right and Mt. Abercrombie (#2: 7,308 feet) to the left.

Looking west, the highest peaks visible in the distance are those of the Kettle Range, 50 to 55 miles away.

Salmo Mountain 15

6,828 Feet

■ Round-Trip Length: **5 miles** ■ Elevation Gain: **908 feet** ■ Hiking Time: **3 hours**

If you're a couch potato looking for a good-sized mountain to climb without all the grunting and hard work, here's the one for you. Because a well-maintained road takes you almost to the top, you can skip the hike and drive.

There's a shuttered fire lookout atop Salmo Mountain which gives purpose to the road. It's passable by low-clearance vehicle the entire way save the last 100 yards.

Though it's an easy climb, getting to Salmo isn't a piece of cake. From Sullivan Lake, it's a 21-mile drive via twisting, switchbacking, gravel and dirt roads. This is a hike that you'll spend more time getting to than doing.

Salmo Mountain is the northernmost mountain on the Top 50 list. Its summit lies just outside the boundaries of the Salmo-Priest Wilderness, a scant two miles from the Canadian border. From the top you'll have a magnificent view of the hundreds of soaring peaks north of the border.

Sure you can drive to the top, but for those purists who believe in making it hard on themselves, the trail description assumes instead of driving, you'll hike the two-and-a-half-mile summit road.

Getting There

■ From the end of the bridge that spans the Pend Oreille River in Metaline Falls, drive north on Highway 31 for 2.1 miles to Sullivan Lake Road (County Road #9345).

■ Turn right and drive 4.9 miles to Forest Service Road #22 (Don't confuse this with Road #2212 which you'll come to first). A sign here lists the mileage to Salmo Mountain, Priest Lake, and East Sullivan Campground.

■ Turn left and drive 6.0 miles until reaching a three-way fork.

■ Bear left onto Road #2220 and drive another 12.8 miles to Road #270, the summit road to Salmo Mountain on the left (Note: If you come to the end of Road 2220, you missed Road 270. Backtrack four-tenths of a mile to find the turnoff.)

The Trail

Salmo Mountain Road #270
Starting Elevation: 5,920 feet
Rating: Easy
Info: Sullivan Lake Ranger District
USGS topo map: Salmo Mountain

Though you'll be hiking on a nicely maintained roadway, the remote location and light use means you'll likely encounter few, if any, vehicles.

From the intersection of Roads 2220 and 270, you'll climb steadily at a gentle pace through a thick forest of Engelmann spruce and subalpine fir. As you climb in elevation, the trees get smaller and unobstructed views more frequent. The road

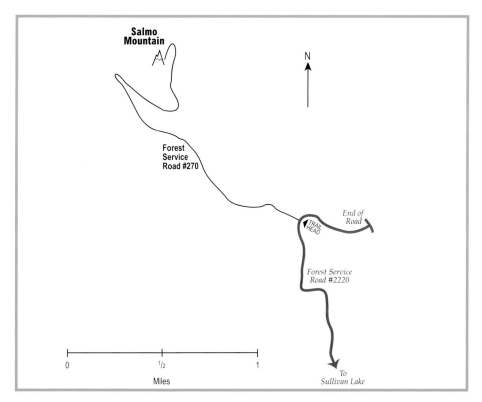

Salmo
Mountain

Forest
Service
Road #270

N

End of
Road

TRAIL
HEAD

Forest Service
Road #2220

0   ¹/₂   1

Miles

To
Sullivan Lake

does a couple switchbacks and you'll soon find yourself on nearly bare slopes with excellent mountain scenery in every direction. Because of the mild slope of the road, this is one of the most pleasant hikes on the list. It's a good one for inviting along friends that would otherwise balk at the idea of climbing a mountain. It takes only 45-50 minutes of steady walking to reach the summit.

From the Summit

Looking to the southwest from the summit, Gypsy Mountain (#1: 7,309 feet), is three miles away, the highest of several bare, pointy peaks on the ridge across the valley. Following the ridge north from Gypsy, the next pointed summit that lies nearly due west from where you stand, a little over two miles away is South Fork (#5: 7,152 feet).

Looking directly south, the neighboring mountain, two miles away and lower in

elevation is Leola Peak (#35: 6,380 feet). To the left of Leola Peak, eight miles distant, the mountain with the burned summit and two bare, rocky patches is Helmer Mountain (#20: 6,734 feet).

Looking east, the many peaks of the Selkirk Range in north Idaho are visible. Lying about five miles due east, the rounded knob protruding from the level ridgeline is Little Snowy Top Mountain in Idaho (6,829 feet). Just left of Little Snowy Top, the taller, three-pronged peak is Snowy Top Mountain (7,572 feet) which lies just south of the Canadian border in Idaho.

Salmo Mountain consists of two peaks. The one with the lookout is the shorter one at 6,828 feet It's only a five-minute walk to the slightly higher north peak. From there you can look down the steep, north-facing slope to the roadless valley below, at the bottom of which flows the Salmo River. The peaks directly across the valley to the north are all in Canada.

16
Molybdenite Mountain

6,784 Feet

■ Round-Trip Length: **5 miles** ■ Elevation Gain: **1,694 feet** ■ Hiking Time: **3 hours**

An intriguing, rock-capped mountain lying just south of Sullivan Lake, Molybdenite is an infrequently-hiked, but easy-to-reach summit. There's some beautiful, subalpine terrain to explore once you reach the peak. However, its lower slopes have been heavily roaded and desecrated by numerous clear-cuts.

An old trail leads to the top of Molybdenite, but it's no longer maintained and is strewn with obstacles. A logging road that comes within a half mile of the summit offers the best route. Once you get beyond the logging road and the clear-cuts, the hike is a fun scramble through stands of subalpine fir and stretches of huge boulders.

Getting There

■ From Ione, drive south on Highway 31 for about one mile to Sullivan Lake Road (County Road 9345). Turn left, crossing the Pend Oreille River, and on the other side of the bridge, go straight, following the road sign to Sullivan Lake.
■ Follow Sullivan Lake Road for 4.3 miles past the bridge to graveled and marked Forest Service Road No. 1933. Turn right and from here it's 8.4 miles to the trailhead.
■ After a half mile, Road #1933 forks. Bear left onto Forest Service Road #1936.
■ Ignore the numerous branch roads and follow this well-maintained gravel road to the trailhead on the left side of the road. Be sure to monitor your mileage since you'll pass at least three similar trailheads before reaching the correct one. The trail is an old logging road, now barricaded. Look for the brown road marker indicating Road No. 1936-100.

The Trail

Forest Service Road 1936-100
Starting Elevation: 5,090 feet
Rating: Break a Sweat
Info: Sullivan Lake Ranger District
USGS topo map: Scotchman Lake

The trailhead is an old logging road that has been gated, prohibiting use by motorized vehicles. Check for the trailhead sign and the brown road marker among the weeds at the trailhead entrance stating that the road is 1936-100.

The trail begins in an old clear-cut and just beyond the gate, after rounding a curve, Molybdenite Mountain will come into view, looming straight ahead.

Ten minutes into the hike you'll leave the clear-cut and enter a timbered section. After another ten or fifteen minutes of walking, you'll enter another clear-cut. At this point you'll be able to catch a good view of Sullivan Lake to the north.

The logging road will soon fork. Take the upper road to your right. A few minutes later the road will reach a saddle between Molybdenite and a low ridge to your right. At this point you'll find a

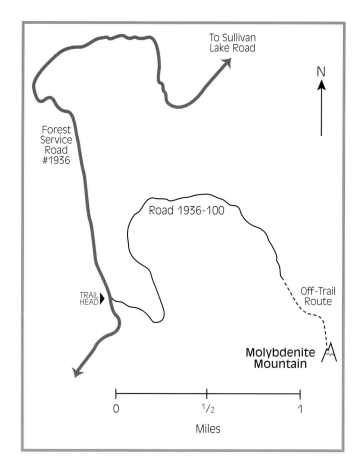

To Sullivan
Lake Road

N

Forest
Service
Road
#1936

Road 1936-100

TRAIL
HEAD ▶

Off-Trail
Route

Molybdenite
Mountain

0   1/2   1

Miles

boulders. They're all part of Molybdenite Mountain, their elevations slightly lower than the main peak.

Looking north, you can see virtually all of Sullivan Lake. The mountain that rises from its east shore, about 6 to 7 miles distant, is Hall Mountain (#39: 6,323 feet). The peak beyond and just to the left of Hall that rises from Sullivan Lake's north end is Sullivan Mountain (#29: 6,483 feet) 12 miles distant.

If you look a little to the left of due north, about 16 to 17 miles distant, you'll see two peaks only a couple miles apart, connected by a ridge. They are Mt. Abercrombie (#2: 7,308 feet) to the left and Mt. Hooknose (#4: 7,210 feet) to the right.

convergence of several logging roads. The summit will be easy to see straight ahead, so take the one road that heads toward it. It will dead-end after ten minutes of walking, forcing you to hoof it off-trail. It's about a half-hour climb from the end of the logging road to the summit.

From the Summit

At the summit you'll find the remains of an old fire lookout tower. There's also a USGS marker listing the elevation as 6,790 feet, six feet higher than current USGS maps.

Looking west, the town of Ione and the Pend Oreille River are easily visible. The range of peaks in the far distance is the Kettle Range west of Colville.

Looking east, there are several nearby peaks capped by fields of rock and

Looking south, the Pend Oreille River is visible again, winding its way through the valley. To the right of due south, the prominent, rounded peak about 21 miles away is Calispell Mountain (#14: 6,855 feet). If the day is clear, you can see the ski runs of 49 Degrees North Ski Area on Chewelah Mountain just beyond and to the left of Calispell Mountain.

A little east of due south, just left of the last visible stretch of the Pend Oreille River, one can see the twin humps of Mt. Spokane and Mt. Kit Carson 45-50 miles away.

Looking roughly southeast, the bright-blue waters of Priest Lake are easily seen.

Columbia Mountain

6,782 Feet
■ Round-Trip Length: **5 miles** ■ Elevation Gain: **1,207 feet** ■ Hiking Time: **4 hours**
(Northwest Forest Pass required)

Columbia Mountain is one of the most accessible climbs on the list. The trailhead lies just off Highway 20 at Sherman Pass, the mountain sits adjacent to the road, and a well-maintained trail takes you to the summit. If you have a friend that you want to "ease" into mountain climbing without turning them off completely, this is a good one to start them on.

Columbia Mountain is in the Kettle Range, situated among several peaks that are over 7,000 feet elevation. The views of these peaks, as well as the lowland valleys to the east and west, are excellent.

Getting There
■ From Kettle Falls, head west on Highway 395, crossing the bridge over the Columbia River.
■ Turn left onto Highway 20 and drive 22.6 miles to the top of Sherman Pass. Turn right at the sign pointing the way to the Kettle Crest Trailhead.

The Trail
Kettle Crest Trail North #13 and
  Columbia Mountain Trail #24.
Starting Elevation: 5,575 feet
Rating: Break a Sweat
Info: Colville Ranger District
USGS topo map: Sherman Peak

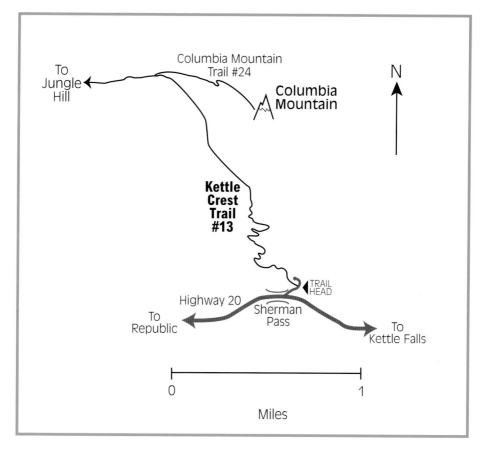

From the trailhead, take the Kettle Crest Trail North #13. It winds up Columbia's south-facing slope before gently ascending the open west-facing slope. It takes about an hour of steady walking to reach the spur trail that goes to the summit. Keep your eyes open because Columbia Mountain Trail #24 angles upward in the opposite direction you're walking. Watch for signs posted on a tree at the intersection. From that point it's about a 3/4-mile walk to the top.

From the Summit

On top you'll find the remains of an old fire lookout that's been knocked down and an old cabin that hasn't. Looking southward across the highway, the next peak over is Sherman Peak (#10: 7,011 feet). The mountain peeking over Sherman's shoulder, three miles away is Snow Peak (#7: 7,103 feet). The pointed, rocky peak beyond Sherman and Snow is Bald Mountain (#11: 6,940 feet), four miles distant.

Looking in the opposite direction to the north, the expansive, grassy-sloped peak next door is Wapaloosie Mountain (#9: 7,018 feet).

Looking southwest, the prominent, rounded peak, 32 miles distant is Moses Mountain (#18: 6,774 feet) on the Colville Indian Reservation. Glancing slightly left of northwest, another rounded, prominent mountain, also about 32 miles away is Bonaparte Mountain (#3: 7,257 feet) in the Okanogan National Forest.

If the day is clear, you may strain your eyes just a bit to see the snow-covered North Cascades far off to the west.

Moses Mountain

6,774 Feet

■ Round-Trip Length: **6 miles** ■ Elevation Gain: **2,089 feet** ■ Hiking Time: **4 hours**

The highest point on the Colville Indian Reservation, Moses Mountain also has the tallest lookout tower of any mountain on the Top 50 list. Still standing since the late '30s or early '40s, the steel tower is still in good shape.

Moses Mountain is like an isolated island in the middle of a wide sea. It's the tallest point for many miles around. You can see far and wide in all directions, from Canada to the Columbia Basin, and from the Cascades to the Kettle Range. This area is rarely visited and it's also a fairly short hike. However, the entire route to the top is via a summit road rather than trail.

Getting There
■ From the Chief Joseph Historical Marker in Nespelem, drive north on Highway 155 for 17.3 miles. You'll have reached and then driven well past the summit of Disautel Pass before coming to a gravel road marked by a weathered sign which reads "Moses L. O.". Turn right here.

■ After crossing the cattle guard, drive 5.5 miles to the start of the summit road which is on the left, marked by a sign.

The Trail
Moses Mountain Look Out Road
Starting Elevation: 4,685 feet
Rating: Break a Sweat
Info: Colville Tribal Headquarters
USGS topo map: Moses Mountain

If you've got a tough, four-wheel-drive vehicle, you can drive all the way to the top. But, assuming you want to do some

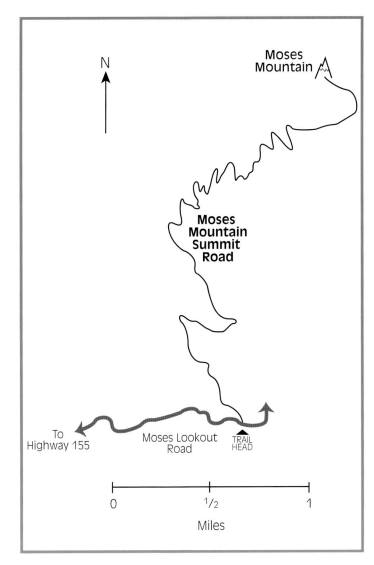

the impression you're almost there. But as you round yet another switchback, you'll find there is still more slope to climb. This is a trick that will make you wonder if the mountain even has a top.

From the Summit

There's an abandoned, all-steel lookout tower atop Moses that is far higher than most towers. Its height was necessary because of the relatively flat summit.

Looking east, you can see the many peaks of the Kettle Crest Range, 30 to 40 miles away. Due east, the flat-topped mountain

hiking, leave your car at the start of the summit road.

As you start your hike, you'll pass through an area that's been selectively logged, but still has plenty of huge, old-growth ponderosa pines.

As you gain elevation, the road switchbacks more frequently, the ponderosas disappear, and the lodgepole and subalpine fir growing here aren't nearly as big. Because Moses has a rounded summit, the steepness of the road will lessen as you approach the top, giving you

about 25 miles away is Grizzly Mountain (#33: 6,397 feet). The prominent mountain lying due north 30 miles away is Mt. Bonaparte (#2: 7,257 feet). Due west, 23 miles away, the towns of Omak and Okanogan are visible in the valley below. Beyond them, the many peaks of the north Cascades are easy to see.

Looking a little to the left of due south, Nespelem is visible, 15 miles distant. Due south, about 35 miles away, flat-topped Steamboat Rock near Grand Coulee is visible, flanked by Banks Lake to the right.

Shedroof Mountain

6,764 Feet

■ Round-Trip Length: **8 miles** ■ Elevation Gain: **844 feet** ■ Hiking Time: **5 hours**

Lying in the Salmo-Priest Wilderness barely a half mile from the Idaho border, Shedroof Mountain is a moderate climb along the little-used, but well-maintained Shedroof Divide Trail. This trail brings you within a half mile of the top, then a rough, unmaintained trail to the former lookout tower takes you the rest of the way.

The entire route is a high-elevation walk through a thick, subalpine forest with occasional openings on south-facing slopes. Huckleberries are numerous in August, but because of its remoteness, human visitors are far less numerous. Berry-picking, solitude, and reflections on the grandeur of nature are perfect opportunities on this hike.

Getting There

■ From the end of the bridge that spans the Pend Oreille River in Metaline Falls, drive 2.1 miles north on Highway 31 to Sullivan Lake Road (County Road #9345).
■ Turn right and drive 4.9 miles to Forest Service Road #22 (Not to be confused with Road #2212 which you'll come to first). A sign listing the mileage to Salmo Mountain, Priest Lake, and East Sullivan Campground is here.
■ Turn left, and you have a quarter mile of pavement, followed by 19 miles of gravel road to the trailhead.
■ Six miles into Road #22, you'll come to a three-way intersection. Bear left, taking Road

#2220 toward Salmo Mountain.
■ At about 13 miles, you'll pass a sign that reads "Shedroof Cut-off Trail #511" This is an alternative route to Shedroof Mountain, though longer and involving a greater elevation gain. For best access to Shedroof, continue on Road #2220 until it terminates at the trailhead.

The Trail

Salmo Divide Trail #535 and Shedroof Divide Trail #512
Starting Elevation: 5,920 feet
Rating: Break a Sweat
Info: Sullivan Lake Ranger District
USGS topo map: Salmo Mountain

There are two trails that originate at the end of Road #2220. Make sure to take Trail 535 which follows an old roadway.

One mile into your hike, the road will narrow to a path, and at this point you should see a mileage sign telling you Shedroof Mountain is three miles away. Just past this spot, there's a spur trail on

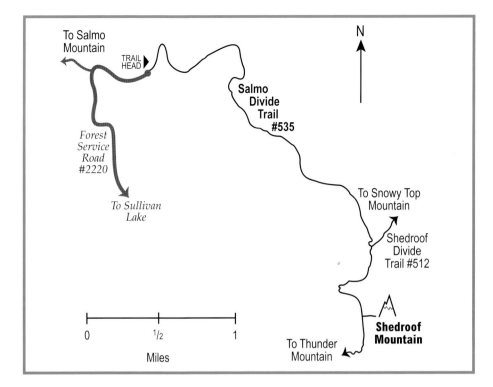

the right that should be ignored.

About one hour into your hike, you'll come around a corner to an open, southwest-facing bald and see Shedroof for the first time. It lies to the south of you, barely a mile away, heavily timbered except for the old clear-cut on its lower northwest-facing slope.

About an hour and a half into the hike you'll come to a saddle where Trail 535 ends as it intersects Trail 512. Turning left, Trail 512 will take you into Idaho and Snowy Top Mountain. But you want to bear right, taking 512 as it switchbacks up the steep, north-facing slope of Shedroof.

Twenty more minutes of hiking will take you to the trail's high point on Shedroof. Here the trail begins to descend the other side, but you'll find the old summit trail on your left. Take it, and though unmaintained and overgrown in places, it's easy to follow, and after another twenty minutes you'll reach the summit of Shedroof.

From the Summit

You'll find the remains of the old lookout tower and cabin here, along with a weathered sign nailed to a stump listing Shedroof's elevation. Looking into the valley to the southeast, both Upper Priest Lake and Priest Lake are easily visible.

Looking nearly due south, the neighboring mountain about 4 miles distant is Thunder Mountain (#24: 6,560 feet). Beyond and just to the left of Thunder, the mountain with two rocky patches and the burned summit is Helmer Mountain (#20: 6,734 feet) about 6 miles away.

Looking westward, the high point on the ridge about 5 miles away, just right of due west, is Gypsy Peak (#1: 7,309 feet).

Also about 5 miles away, the prominent peak to the northeast is Snowy Top Mountain (7,572 feet) in Idaho. Everywhere you look, eastward into Idaho or northward into Canada, you can see the numerous peaks that make up the Selkirk Mountains.

Helmer Mountain

6,734 Feet
◼ Round-Trip Length: **9 miles** ◼ Elevation Gain: **1,334 feet** ◼ Hiking Time: **5 hours**

Helmer Mountain lies along the Shedroof Divide in the Salmo-Priest Wilderness. It's a moderately long day hike that takes you up and down the slopes of two other mountains on the Top 50 list along the way. They too can be scaled without adding much time to your hike.

Helmer was hit by fire in the summer of 1994, burning about 1000 acres at the summit. However, the route to the top passes through only a small section of the burn. Because of the short growing season at this elevation, very little vegetation has grown back, leaving the summit black and barren, giving it an eerie, other-worldly appearance.

The trail is well-maintained and easy to follow, yet lightly used. In the entire Salmo-Priest trail system, encounters with other hikers range from never to very infrequent.

Getting There

◼ This hike uses the same trailhead as #23 Mankato Mountain and #31 Round Top Mountain From the end of the bridge spanning the Pend Oreille River in Metaline Falls, drive 2.1 miles north on Highway 31 until reaching Sullivan Lake Road (County Road #9345).

◼ Turn right and drive 4.9 miles to Forest Service Road #22 (Don't confuse this

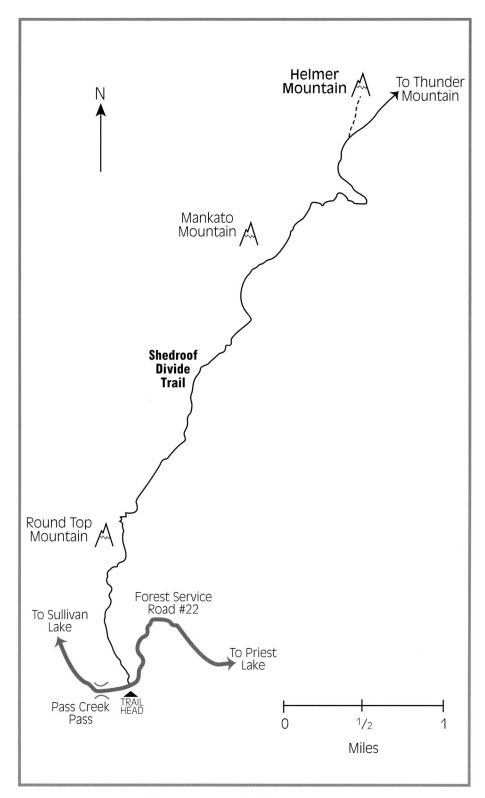

N

Helmer Mountain

To Thunder Mountain

Mankato Mountain

Shedroof Divide Trail

Round Top Mountain

Forest Service Road #22

To Sullivan Lake

To Priest Lake

Pass Creek Pass

TRAIL HEAD

0   1/2   1

Miles

with Road #2212 which you'll come to first). You should see a sign listing the mileage to Priest Lake, Salmo Mountain, and East Sullivan Campground. From this point it's a quarter mile of pavement followed by 14 miles of gravel road to the trailhead.

■ Six miles into Road #22 you'll reach a three-way fork. Bear right.

■ Stay on Road #22 and proceed an additional 8.4 miles toward Pass Creek Pass.

■ At the pass summit you'll find a sign listing the mileage to Nordman and Priest River, Idaho. Barely two-tenths of a mile down the other side, you'll find the trailhead sign, and just past it, a pullout on the right with parking for two cars. If it's full, use the ample area at the pass summit to park.

The Trail

Shedroof Divide Trail #512
Starting Elevation: 5,400 feet
Rating: Huffin' & Puffin'
Info: Sullivan Lake Ranger District
USGS topo map: Pass Creek

From Pass Creek Pass, the Shedroof Divide Trail ascends Round Top Mountain, which sits adjacent to the pass. After 40 to 50 minutes of steady walking through a mix of timber stands, recent burns, and open grass, the trail reaches its high point on Round Top. At this point you'll find a spur trail which goes to the summit (it may be hard to see because of a downed tree). Take this short trail to the summit if desired. If not, continue on as the main trail descends Round Top's back side.

The trail will soon level out and generally stay that way until entering an old burn marked by a profusion of lifeless, gray snags. At this point, you can see Mankato Mountain with its bald summit lying straight ahead. The trail will soon reach a saddle and switch from a west-facing slope to an east-facing slope as it

begins descending Mankato. If you want to top Mankato, leave the trail before it begins descending. Otherwise, stay on the trail as it descends until making a 90-degree turn, going from Mankato's east slope onto Helmer's south-facing slope. From here the trail will soon begin ascending. You'll do a switchback and come to a fork where a spur trail leads steeply to the right. Avoid this trail which soon disappears on a subsidiary peak of Helmer.

Even young hikers will find some of Eastern Washington's highest peaks easy to climb.

The trail will level out somewhat as it comes to the area burned by the 1994 fire. At this point you'll be able to see Helmer's summit which has been obscured until now. As you're walking through this blackened, lifeless landscape, you'll see the trail veer to the right, away from the summit, cutting across Helmer's east-facing slope. Leave the trail at this point and follow the moderately pitched ridgeline to the summit. You should reach the top within 15 minutes.

Blossoms of arrowleaf balsamroot, a common sight in the lowlands of Eastern Washington.

From the Summit

Despite the fire, there are lots of trees still standing on Helmer's broad, relatively flat summit. This restricts the views somewhat, but if you wander around the top,

A pair of coyote pups patiently wait for mom to bring home some food.

you can find openings that allow vistas of the surrounding country.

Looking east, the impressive, pointed peaks of the Selkirk Mountain Range in north Idaho are easy to see. Visible too, in the valley between yourself and the Selkirks, is the gleaming waters of Upper Priest Lake.

Looking back in the direction you came from, neighboring Mankato Mountain (#23: 6,590 feet) is barely a mile away. Beyond Mankato, three miles distant, is Round Top (#31: 6,466 feet). If you wander to the north end of the summit, Thunder Mountain (#24: 6,560 feet) is the neighboring peak to the north, a little over two miles away.

Glancing just to the right of due west, seven miles away you'll see Sullivan Mountain (#29: 6,483 feet) and if you look hard, the lookout tower that sits at its summit.

Midnight Mountain

6,660 Feet
■ Round-Trip Length: **5 miles** ■ Elevation Gain: **1,160 feet** ■ Hiking Time: **3 hours**

Here's yet another peak in the Kettle Range, one of 22 on the Top 50 list. Though the upper slopes of Midnight Mountain will have to be traversed without benefit of a trail, the way is fairly easy, and the hiking time is short, allowing plenty of time to conquer nearby peaks, if desired.

The trail to reach this peak was originally constructed in 1892 as a stagecoach road. At the time, it was the only road that connected the upper Columbia River Valley to points on the coast.

The trailhead for this hike is the same used for Copper Butte (#6) and Lambert Mountain (#28).

Getting There
■ From Kettle Falls, drive west on Highway 395 across the Columbia River and turn left onto Highway 20.

■ Drive 18.4 miles to Albion Hill Road #2030.

■ Turn right onto this well-maintained gravel road and drive 7.3 miles to the sign marking the parking lot and trailhead of the Old Stage Road Trail #75.

The Trail
Old Stage Road Trail #75 and Kettle Crest Trail #13.
Starting Elevation: 5,500 feet
Rating: Break a Sweat
Info: Kettle Falls Ranger District
USGS topo map: Copper Butte

From the trailhead, the path ascends gently through a thick forest. After about 20 minutes, you'll enter a burn that resulted from a 1994 fire. After another 15 minutes of walking, you'll reach the saddle

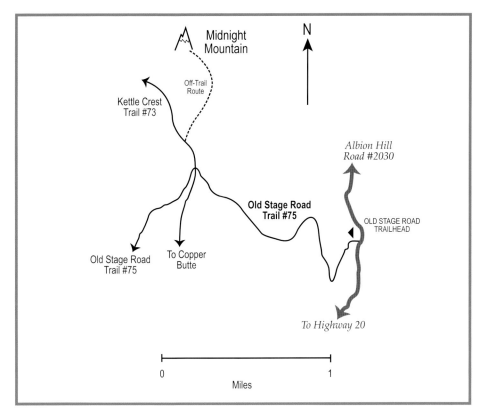

between Copper Butte to the left (south) and Midnight Mountain to the right (north). The Old Stage Road Trail begins descending from here. Leave it and take the Kettle Crest Trail which heads uphill to your right. A sign on a blackened tree marks the barely decipherable trail, which gets better past the saddle.

Take the Kettle Crest Trail for less than a quarter mile until it exits the woods and comes to an open, grassy slope. At this point, you're on the south slope of Midnight Mountain, where the way to the top is the easiest. Leave the trail here and head up the moderately steep, open slope. After leaving the trail, it's a 30- to 40-minute hike to the top.

From the Summit

Though the south-facing slope is green and partially timbered, the summit was burned in the 1994 fire. Because of this, good views are possible, especially looking westward toward the Curlew Lake Valley.

Looking southward, the summit of Copper Butte (#6: 7,140 feet) lies a mile and a half away. U S Mountain (#44: 6,232 feet) lies across the valley to the east, its summit about two and a half miles away.

Looking just a little to the right of due west, the prominent, rounded mountain 30 miles distant is Mt. Bonaparte (#3: 7,257 feet) in the Okanogan National Forest.

Looking to the southwest, another rounded, prominent mountain visible in the distance is Moses Mountain ((#18: 6,774 feet) on the Colville Indian Reservation. Its summit is about 36 miles from your vantage point.

If you have the time, it's an easy walk to Lambert Mountain (#28: 6,525 feet) which lies due north. Just follow the gently descending ridge northward for about 3/4 of a mile to the summit.

King Mountain

6,634 Feet

■ Round-Trip Length: **6 miles** ■ Elevation Gain: **1,184 feet** ■ Hiking Time: **4 hours**

This mountain in the Kettle Range is a thickly treed, seldom visited place that can be reached by a rough, little-used, dirt road that goes all the way to the summit.

The route to King Mountain, though not overly long, takes you up and down a couple ridgelines that are like hurdles in your way. This adds three or four hundred feet to the elevation difference between the trailhead and the top.

The summit of King can't be seen until late in the hike as you clear the last ridge. Arriving at the summit, the views are limited because of a thick stand of lodgepole pine. However, a subsidiary peak just a short walk away gives you an unobstructed view in all directions.

Getting There

■ From Kettle Falls, head west on Highway 395 across the Columbia. After crossing the bridge, turn left onto Highway 20 and drive 18.4 miles to Albion Hill Road #2030.

■ Turn right and drive 4.9 miles (passing the Wapaloosie Mountain Trailhead) to the trailhead.

■ The King Mountain trailhead is actually a branch road on the right. There's no trailhead sign, so keep your eyes open. You'll find the trailhead consists of two separate, marked roads with a common starting point. The obvious one, Road #200, is not the one you want. To the right of it is the less obvious Road #460. Take it to reach King Mountain.

The Trail

Forest Service Road #460
Starting Elevation: 5,450 feet
Rating: Break a Sweat
Info: Colville Ranger District
USGS topo map: Copper Butte

The trail to King's summit is a rough jeep road that's open to off-road vehicles. However usage is so light there's little chance you'll see either man or machine.

Road 460 begins right away with switchbacks as it ascends the first ridge on King's west slope. The forest through here is mostly pine and Douglas fir and offers few views until you reach the ridge crest and a more open landscape.

After approximately thirty minutes of steady walking, you'll descend slightly from the first ridge crest and pass through a thickly treed north-facing slope which soon begins ascending the next ridge. The road swings northeasterly as it climbs the low point of the ridge, then begins to descend.

It's shortly after negotiating this

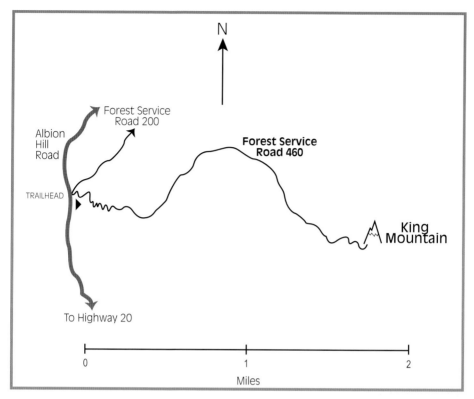

second ridge that you'll get a glimpse of King's summit for the first time. The trail levels out in the wide saddle between the ridge just traversed and the summit ahead. A thick, uniform forest of 15- to 25-foot, small-diameter lodgepole pine dominates this area, a growth indicative of past fire history.

The road ascends the summit, getting steeper as it nears the top. It switchbacks just before topping the rather unspectacular summit.

From the Summit

Upon reaching the summit you'll find that views are limited because of the thick stand of lodgepole. However, another high point about a half-mile to the east is easily visible. This rocky butte is a subsidiary peak of King Mountain, one foot lower in elevation than the main peak. But because of its rocky, treeless summit, it offers better views. To reach it, follow the road which continues along the ridge until it forks. Bear left and climb until this spur road ends. You'll have about 100 feet of walking from the end of the road to the top.

Looking back from where you came, the mountain that rises above King Mountain, three miles distant, lying almost due west, is Scar Mountain. (#8: 7,046 feet). Looking to the right of Scar, the next-door mountain is Copper Butte (#6: 7,140 feet).

Looking roughly southwest, the mountain with the broad summit and open upper slopes, also about three miles away, is Wapaloosie Mountain (#9: 7,018 feet). South of Wapaloosie, peaks of the southern section of the Kettle Crest on the other side of Highway 20 are also visible.

If you walk to the east end of your vantage point, you'll see a lower-elevation, rounded mountain with a broad, gently-sloped summit that lies next to King. This is Mack Mountain (#46: 6,196 feet).

Mankato Mountain

6,590 Feet

■ Round-Trip Length: **7 miles** ■ Elevation Gain: **1,190 feet** ■ Hiking Time: **4 hours**

This is one of several peaks in the Salmo-Priest Wilderness that sits right at the border separating protected wilderness from clear-cut National Forest land. However, the trail stays entirely within the Salmo-Priest Wilderness, passing through old burns and dense forest much of the way.

A moderate length hike, Mankato is reached via the lightly used Shedroof Divide Trail to within a half mile of the peak. An easy, off-trail climb up an open, grassy slope will bring you to the summit.

To reach Mankato, you'll walk right by the summit of #31 Round Top Mountain. A twenty-minute diversion will allow you to bag Round Top in addition to Mankato Mountain.

Getting There

■ This hike uses the same trailhead as #20 Helmer Mountain and #31 Round Top Mountain. From the end of the bridge spanning the Pend Oreille River in Metaline Falls, drive 2.1 miles on Highway 31 to Sullivan Lake Road (County Rd. 9345).

■ Turn right and drive 4.9 miles to Forest Service Road #22 (Don't be confused by Road #2212 which you'll come to first). Turn left where a sign listing the distance to Priest Lake, Salmo Mountain, and East Sullivan Campground points the way. The first quarter mile of Road #22 is paved, the next 14 miles are gravel.

■ Six miles into Road #22 you'll come to a three-way fork. Bear right, staying on Road #22, and drive 8.4 additional miles to just beyond the top of Pass Creek Pass.

■ There's a sign at the pass summit which gives the mileage to Nordman and Priest River, Idaho. Barely two-tenths of a mile down the other side you'll see the trailhead sign, and just beyond it, a pull-out on the right for two cars to park. If the pullout is full, there's ample parking at the pass summit.

The Trail

Shedroof Divide Trail #512
Starting Elevation: 5,400 feet
Rating: Break a Sweat
Info: Sullivan Lake Ranger District
USGS topo map: Pass Creek

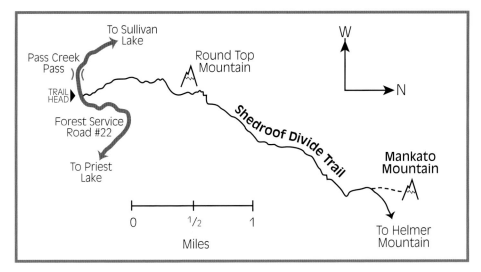

The Shedroof Divide Trail will take you through a recently burned area as you ascend the south slope of Round Top Mountain. Past the burn, you'll walk through a thickly treed area before entering the open, grassy slopes of upper Round Top Mountain. The trail will reach its high point on Round Top after 40 to 50 minutes of hiking and begin to descend. At this point there's a spur trail heading upward on the left, though a recently blown-down tree obscures the trail junction. As a sidetrip, you can take this spur trail and be at the top of Round Top within ten minutes. Otherwise, continue on the Shedroof Divide Trail as it descends Round Top.

The trail will soon level out and stay that way for the next mile or so until you enter an old burn marked by a profusion of bare, gray snags. As you are walking through this area, you're approaching Mankato which lies straight ahead nearly due north. The trail, which is on a west-facing slope, will soon reach a saddle and cross over to descend the east-facing slope of Mankato. Leave the trail before it starts to descend and continue walking northward as you climb Mankato. The first 50 yards are a little brushy after leaving the trail. But thereafter, it's just ankle-deep bunchgrass. You may find an old, unmaintained trail which comes and goes as you ascend. Within fifteen minutes you should be at the top.

From the Summit

Look for a gray snag that's nearest the summit. You can verify you've reached Mankato by finding the old, weathered, partially burned sign nailed to it that lists the mountain's elevation.

Looking to the north, the peak with the burned summit barely a mile away is Helmer Mountain (#20: 6,734 feet). Looking in the opposite direction to the south, the next-door peak at about the same elevation is Round Top (#31: 6,466 feet) which you passed by earlier. Looking across the valley, just left of due north, the bald, pointy peak eight miles distant that juts highest among the other points along the ridge line is Gypsy Mountain (#1: 7,309 feet).

The rocky range of mountains to the east are the Selkirks of North Idaho.

Mankato actually consists of three peaks. You can see a ridge that runs west from the main peak. Walking this ridge will take you to the two subsidiary peaks which are slightly higher in elevation than the main peak.

Thunder Mountain

6,560 Feet

■ Round-Trip Length: **14 miles** ■ Elevation Gain: **2,400 feet** ■ Hiking Time: **7 hours**

This long hike will take you through the best and the worst that Colville National Forest has to offer.

Thunder Mountain lies within the boundaries of the Salmo-Priest Wilderness. However the trailhead is outside the wilderness area and a lengthy portion of the trail passes through a huge clear-cut. Once you're past it though, the trail enters a stand of large-diameter, old-growth trees, unmatched by any other climb on the Top 50 list. The huge, soaring behemoths will leave your mouth agape as you stare upward at their immense, arrow-straight trunks. The dark, shadowy landscape beneath these giants is reminiscent of a rain forest. This hike is one of the more rousing, breathtaking ones on the list.

Getting There

■ From the end of the bridge spanning the Pend Oreille River in Metaline Falls, drive 2.1 miles north on Highway 31 and turn right onto Sullivan Lake Road (County Road #9345)

■ Drive 4.9 miles to Forest Service Road #22 (Ignore Road #2212 which you'll come to first). A sign listing the mileage to Priest Lake, Salmo Mountain, and East Sullivan Campground points the way. Turn left and from here you have 12 miles of graveled road to the trailhead.

■ At six miles you'll come to a three-way fork. Bear left onto Forest Service Road #2220 and drive another six miles to signed Thunder Creek Trailhead #526 on the right.

The Trail

Thunder Creek Trail #526 and Shedroof Divide Trail #512

Starting Elevation: 4,160 feet

Rating: Major Workout

Info: Sullivan Lake Ranger District

USGS topo map: Helmer Mountain

Leaving the trailhead, Thunder Creek Trail #526 ascends through a thick forest of tall hemlocks via an old roadbed. After 3/4 of a mile, you'll reach a clear-cut which you'll spend about a mile and a half walking through until entering an old-growth section that contrasts sharply with the open clear-cut. Enormous hemlocks and cedars block much of the sun, leaving a shadowy, lightly vegetated understory sheltered from wind and light.

The trail through here is well-constructed, and in several places it is boardwalk or raised earth as it passes through wet areas. It's a magnificent section which should be passed through slowly and with plenty of pauses for admiration.

After five miles of walking, Trail 526 reaches a steep-sided saddle and intersects Shedroof Divide Trail #512 in the middle of a hairpin loop, giving the appearance there's a convergence of three trails instead of two. Turn left, following

■ *Thunder Mountain*

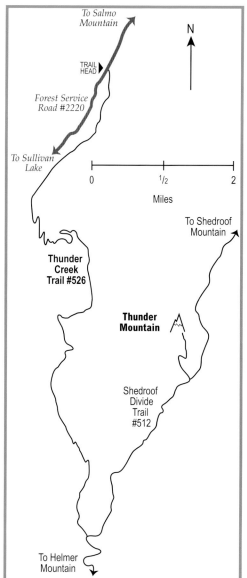

summit. The main trail heads north, following the top of a flat ridgeline. As the trail cuts to the east-facing side of the ridge, it will begin to descend. Just before it starts descending, you'll find the unmaintained, unmarked spur trail on the left. Watch for it or you may miss it.

The spur trail switchbacks up Thunder Mountain's south-facing slope. Though unmaintained, the trail is in good shape and easily discernable. Once on the summit trail, the top can be reached in 20 minutes.

From the Summit

The remains of an old fire lookout are at the top. Posted on a tree near the concrete supports, you'll find a weathered sign that states the elevation of Thunder Mountain.

Trees obscure your views near the old lookout. However, you'll find the southern end of the summit open, affording unobstructed views, especially to the east. You'll also find the remains of an old cabin which housed the lookout personnel.

From here you have an excellent view of Upper Priest Lake in the valley below and beyond it, the craggy Selkirk Range of north Idaho. Unfortunately you'll also have a great view of the plentiful and too-common Idaho clear-cut.

Looking southward, the next-door peak with the burnt summit and two bare, rocky areas on the north-facing slope is Helmer Mountain (#20: 6,734 feet).

Looking roughly northwest toward the ridge across the valley, the bare, rocky peak, about six miles distant, tallest among the other peaks along the ridge is Gypsy Mountain (#1: 7,309 feet).

If you can find a clearing to see due west, Sullivan Mountain (#29: 6,483 feet) and its summit lookout is visible eight miles away.

the weathered sign on a tree that points the way to Thunder Mountain.

The trail ascends steeply for 1/4 mile then levels out for about 3/4 miles of easy walking. The trail will begin ascending again and about 30 minutes past the trail intersection, you'll get a glimpse of the partially open summit of Thunder Mountain ahead, which up to now has been obscured from view. About 35 to 40 minutes past the trail intersection, you'll come to the spur trail which leads to the

Edds Mountain 25

6,550 Feet

■ Round-Trip Length: **5 miles** ■ Elevation Gain: **1,650 feet** ■ Hiking Time: **3 hours**

This mountain in the Kettle Crest Range is easy to reach and requires only a moderate hike to top-out. Yet few hikers make it a destination.

Most of Edds' upper slopes consist of gray, lifeless snags that resulted from the White Mountain Fire of 1988. But the route up traverses a slope that escaped most of the devastation.

The unmaintained trail to Edds is so sporadically used that it's hard to decipher in places. The occasional horseman taking this trail, leaving obvious bare-dirt patches inflicted by horseshoes, is the only thing keeping the trail from being swallowed up by the relentless advance of grasses and brush.

Mount Edds' proximity to #11 Bald Mountain can make conquering both peaks in one hike a possibility.

Getting There

■ From Kettle Falls, drive west on Highway 395 across the Columbia River and turn left onto Highway 20.
■ Drive 22.6 miles to the top of Sherman Pass. From the crest of the pass, continue down the other side another 9.9 miles to marked Hall Creek Road.
■ Turn left on this well-maintained gravel road and drive another 4.5 miles to Edds Road, which is also marked as Forest Service Road #300.
■ Turn left, immediately crossing a cattleguard, in front of which you should see a brown road marker indicating you're on Forest Service Road #300. The trailhead is at the end of the road, three miles distant. But you'll have to walk the last mile unless you have a high-clearance vehicle.

The Trail

Edds Mountain Trail #3.
Starting elevation: 4,900 feet
Rating: Break a Sweat
Info: Colville Ranger District
USGS topo map: Edds Mountain

Edds Mountain Trail #3 begins at the end of Edds Road No. 300. There's no trailhead sign, nor any indication that there's a hiking trail. However the trail is easy to find and appears well-maintained, at the beginning at least.

The trail climbs gently through a forest of Douglas fir and tamarack. After 3/4 of a mile, you'll come to an area of tall grasses

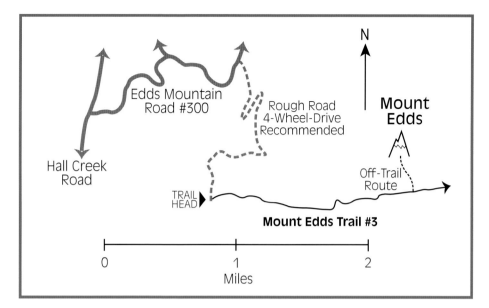

where the trail may be hard to follow. Keep heading up in the same general direction and after a couple hundred feet you should find the trail reappearing beyond the tall grasses.

Soon the trail becomes steeper and traverses past rock outcrops and sections of half-buried boulders. The trail may be hard to see now and then, but it can be quickly rediscovered.

About an hour into the hike, you'll find the trail leveling out as it nears the summit of Edds Mountain. However the trail skirts by the summit without topping it. Leave the trail before it begins descending to connect with the Kettle Crest Trail a couple miles to the east. It's about a ten-minute hike to the summit after leaving the trail.

From the Summit

The summit of Edds Mountain is long and ridgelike. After leaving the trail, you'll have to walk to the far (north) end to reach the high point which is marked by a small rock outcrop. Here you'll be above the burnt gray snags and shoulder-high saplings coming up to replace them.

Looking nearly due east, a bit less than two miles away, the next-door mountain, rocky and rounded, is Bald Mountain (#11: 6,940 feet). If you have the time, the Edds Mountain Trail will take you to Bald if you wish to climb it.

Looking to the left of Bald Mountain, the fire-scarred mountain with three distinct summit humps three miles away is Snow Mountain (#7: 7,103 feet).

Looking to the right of Bald Mountain, the fire-scarred mountain with the ridge-like summit, also about three miles away is Barnaby Buttes (#27: 6,534 feet). And to the right of Barnaby, the rocky, fire-scarred mountain, about five miles distant, is White Mountain (#12: 6,921 feet).

Turning your gaze westward, a little to the left of due west, the prominent, rounded mountain, about 28 miles distant is Moses Mountain (#18: 6,774 feet) on the Colville Indian Reservation. Looking northwest, another prominent, rounded mountain, completely timbered, about 31 miles away is Bonaparte Mountain (#3: 7,257 feet).

If the day is clear, looking far in the distance to the west, you can see the many jagged and snow-capped peaks of the North Cascades.

Jungle Hill

6,544 Feet

■ Round-Trip Length: **10 miles** ■ Elevation Gain: **2,234 feet** ■ Hiking Time: **7 hours**

This "hill" in the Kettle Range is easily overlooked because of the prominent, higher-elevation peaks nearby. However, the moderate-length hike takes the same effort, and provides the same satisfaction and scenery that its higher neighbors provide.

Taking the Jungle Hill Trail and the Kettle Crest Trail brings you close to the summit, leaving an easy fifteen-minute off-trail hike to reach the top.

One of the satisfactions of climbing Jungle Hill is finding little evidence of human visitation at the summit. Though it can't be verified, it's possible an entire hiking season may pass without a single person arriving at the top. Knowing that you're a rare visitor, stepping on ground that may have been untrampled for years brings a special feeling. Though humans have criss-crossed the nation with roads and ventured deep into forests to build towns and homes, there are still wild places close-by where human activity and the taming of nature are absent, and those inclined to seek the magical allure of the natural world still have a place to go.

Getting There

■ From Kettle Falls, drive west on Highway 395, crossing the Columbia River. At the end of the bridge, turn left onto Highway 20.
■ Drive 18.4 miles toward Sherman Pass until reaching Albion Hill Road #2030.
■ Turn right onto Albion Hill Road and drive seven-tenths of a mile over a good gravel road to the signed Jungle Hill Trailhead.

The Trail

Jungle Hill Trail #16 and Kettle Crest Trail North #13
Starting elevation: 4,310 feet
Rating: Huffin' & Puffin
Info: Colville Ranger District
USGS topo map: Copper Butte

Jungle Hill Trail #16 parallels Sherman Creek in its early reaches and intersects Trail 82 to Sherman Pass just beyond the trailhead. Stay on Trail 16 by going straight, crossing the creek.

The hike climbs moderately as it follows the creek, but soon veers away and begins climbing a steep hillside. After a series of switchbacks, you'll come to a rock outcrop and get a good view of your destination. Jungle Hill lies to the west, a couple miles away. Left of Jungle Hill you'll also get a good view of neighboring Columbia Mountain (#17: 6,782 feet)

After two hours of climbing, the trail will intersect Kettle Crest Trail #13. At this point you're on the south shoulder of Wapaloosie Mountain. Turn left and from here it's about an hour and a half to the summit of Jungle Hill.

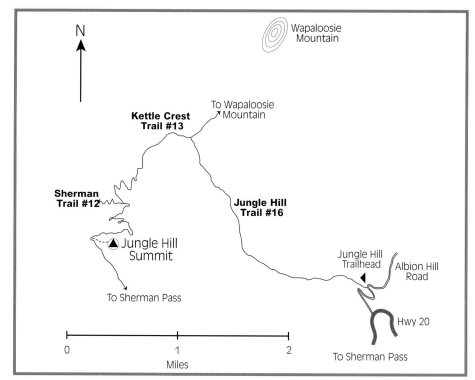

After another half hour of hiking, the Kettle Crest Trail will bottom out at the saddle between Wapaloosie and Jungle Hill. Here you'll find another spur trail which should be ignored. Take the Kettle Crest Trail as it switchbacks up Jungle Hill's steep, north-facing slope. About a half hour beyond the saddle, the trail will reach its high point on Jungle Hill, leveling out as it makes a wide turn, leaving the north-facing slope and coming to the southwest-facing slope. Here it will begin to descend slightly, your signal to leave the trail and climb uphill through the trees. The incline here is moderate, and there's little underbrush to impede your walking. Within fifteen minutes you should be at the top.

From the Summit

There's nothing at the summit to confirm you've reached the top of Jungle Hill save a single small rock cairn. Because there's a stand of lodgepole pine at the top, the views are obstructed. But continue walking the same direction as you were when approaching the summit, going down the other side a short distance. You'll come to an open bald that'll allow a panoramic view. Here you'll be able to see the open, grassy slopes of Wapaloosie Mountain (#9: 7,018 feet) lying a couple miles to the north. Looking the opposite direction, Columbia Mountain (#17: 6,782 feet) lies a mile and a half to the south. Looking roughly northeast, the twin-peaked mountain across the valley, about 5 to 6 miles distant, is King Mountain (#22: 6,634 feet).

If you've got time, you can get back on the Kettle Crest Trail and climb Columbia Mountain. Or if you're in an adventurous mood, go off-trail and follow the ridge that connects the two mountains. There's little vegetation under the thick tree cover, and you'll find an old trail going up Columbia's north-facing slope that leads to numerous rocky buttes that invite climbing and exploration.

Barnaby Buttes

27

6,534 Feet

■ Round-Trip Length: **6 miles** ■ Elevation Gain: **2,034 feet** ■ Hiking Time: **4 hours**

Barnaby Buttes, at the southern end of the Kettle Crest Range, is reached by a moderate length day hike. As recently as the 1970s, there was a manned lookout tower at the summit. It's now torn down, and the jeep road that serviced it has become the trail.

There are several trailheads hikers can use to reach Barnaby Buttes, but the route described here, approaching from the east, is the shortest.

Despite the numerous, well-maintained trails, Barnaby Buttes is an infrequently visited place, as nearly all mountains in the Kettle Range.

Getting There

■ From Kettle Falls, drive westward on Highway 395 across the Columbia River. Turn left onto State Highway 20 after crossing the bridge.

■ Drive 10.4 miles to graveled South Sherman Creek Road #2020 which should be marked by a sign. Turn left.

■ Drive 6.5 miles until reaching a fork. Bear left onto Barnaby Creek Road #2014.

■ Just three-tenths of a mile into Road #2014 you'll see the trailhead sign for Barnaby Buttes and the Kettle Crest Trail. Turn right onto this road (Forest Service Road #500) and if your vehicle is high clearance, drive to the trailhead at the end of the road. If your vehicle does not handle oil pan-scraping humps so well, park here and walk the mile and a half to the trailhead.

The Trail

Barnaby Buttes Trail #70 and Kettle Crest Trail #13.
Starting elevation: 4,500 feet
Rating: Break a Sweat
Info: Colville Ranger District
USGS topo map: Sherman Peak

As mentioned earlier, the Barnaby Buttes Trail is an old jeep road now off-limits to

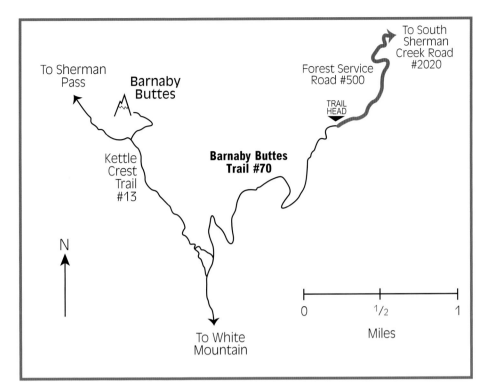

To Sherman Pass

Barnaby Buttes

To South Sherman Creek Road #2020

Forest Service Road #500

TRAIL HEAD

Kettle Crest Trail #13

Barnaby Buttes Trail #70

N

To White Mountain

0 ½ 1

Miles

motorized vehicles. The trail ascends moderately, switchbacking up the steep upper slopes until reaching the top of the Kettle Crest ridge where it turns northward.

The trail along the ridge is level or slightly ascending as you approach the summit, but soon you'll begin climbing Barnaby's south-facing slope. Along this stretch, you may find the Kettle Crest Trail which runs parallel to the old jeep road. Eventually, the two paths merge.

A bit less than a mile of walking along the Kettle Crest Trail will bring you to the trail's high point on Barnaby. You should see the spur trail on the right leading to the summit, and a sign nailed to a tree marking the way. If you start going steeply downhill, you've missed it. Once on the spur trail, you should arrive at the summit in less than ten minutes.

From the Summit

At the summit, you'll find concrete supports and a stairway left from the old lookout tower. Looking northward, Snow Peak (#7: 7,103 feet) is the mountain looming almost due north, three miles away. One mile beyond, poking its tip up just behind Snow Peak is Sherman Peak (#10: 7,011 feet). Looking to the northwest, three miles away is Edds Mountain (#25: 6,550 feet) with a thick forest of burnt gray snags on its east-facing slope. A couple miles away, the jutting peak between Snow Peak and Edds Mountain is Bald Mountain (#11: 6,940 feet).

Looking roughly southeast, the neighboring mountain with a broad, rocky summit two miles distant, is White Mountain (#12: 6,921 feet).

Barnaby Buttes is so named because of the numerous rocky buttes which crop out along the edges of the relatively flat summit. These buttes are fun to explore and provide excellent vistas. Spend a little time wandering around and checking out the landscape.

Lambert Mountain

28

6,525 Feet
Round-Trip Length: **6 miles** ▪ Elevation Gain: **1,025 feet** ▪ Hiking Time: **4 hrs**

Here's another two-for-one-deal. In order to bag the summit of Lambert Mountain, you'll first have to climb #21 Midnight Mountain. About half the route to Lambert is off-trail. However, it's easy walking through a mostly open landscape.

Lambert is located in the loftiest section of the Kettle Crest. Just to the south are three 7,000-footers including #6 Copper Butte, the highest peak in the Kettles at 7,140 feet If you're the ambitious sort and get an early start, it's possible to bag Midnight Mountain, Mt. Lambert, and the three 7,000-footers all in one day.

Getting There

▪ This hike utilizes the same trailhead as #6 Copper Butte and #21 Midnight Mountain. From Kettle Falls, drive west on Highway 395 across the Columbia River. After crossing the bridge, turn left onto Highway 20.

▪ Drive 18.4 miles to Albion Hill Road #2030. Turn right and take this graveled road for 7.7 miles to the signed Old Stage Road Trailhead.

The Trail

Old Stage Road Trail #75 and Kettle
 Crest Trail #13
Starting elevation: 5,500 feet
Rating: Break a Sweat
Info: Colville Ranger District
USGS topo map: Copper Butte

The route to Lambert Mountain is the same as #21 Midnight Mountain. Take the Old Stage Road Trail for about 40 minutes until it reaches its high point at the saddle between Copper Butte and Midnight Mountain. Instead of following Old Stage Trail down the other side, turn right and take the Kettle Crest Trail for about a quarter mile until it comes out of a stand of timber to a grassy slope. Leave the trail here and amble up the moderately steep slope until reaching the summit of Midnight Mountain. This should take 30 to 40 minutes after leaving the trail.

From Midnight Mountain, continue walking in a northerly direction, staying atop the ridge as it gently descends through the burned and black landscape which resulted from a 1994 fire. The walking is easy and you may find an old, unmaintained trail which comes and goes.

▪ *Lambert Mountain*

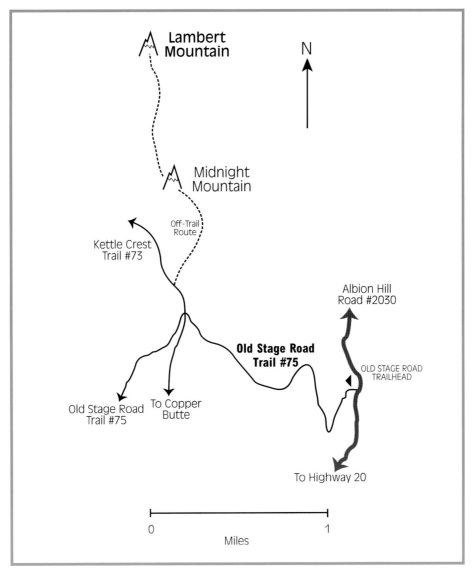

The saddle between Midnight and Lambert mountains is very shallow, so after bottoming out, you'll begin climbing a short and very easy slope until reaching the summit. The walk from Midnight Mountain to Lambert takes less than 30 minutes.

From the Summit

Mt. Lambert was ravaged by the 1994 Copper Butte Fire. Its summit and south slope are completely blackened. This area is a popular hangout for mule deer bedding down during daylight hours. Watch for them as you traverse the trail from Midnight Mountain.

Mt. Lambert is off the beaten path, and thus rarely visited. There's little sign of human visitation, and there's no signage indicating you've reached the summit.

Even though the mountaintop has been burned, Lambert is so thickly treed with snags that there's no good spot for viewing.

Sullivan Mountain

29

6,483 Feet
■ Round-Trip Length: **16 miles** ■ Elevation Gain: **924 feet** ■ Hiking Time: **9 hours**

Here's a mountain sitting at the edge of the Salmo-Priest Wilderness that can be reached from two different trailheads, offering hikes that range from one extreme to the other. For the trail-toughened, a daylong hike of 16 miles from the Bear Pasture Trailhead along Crowell Ridge takes you to Sullivan Mountain and back. For the couch potato, the rough lookout road brings you within a quarter mile of the top. Taking this route, you'll probably get a more rigorous workout pushing on the brake pedal as you drive back down. The trail description, however, assumes you'll do the longer hike.

Sullivan Mountain is one of only a handful on the list which has a still-standing lookout tower at the summit.

Be aware that the road leading to the Bear Pasture Trailhead is closed on August 15th of each year for wildlife considerations.

Since you'll hike the length of Crowell Ridge, you can easily take a short diversion to climb the high point of #13 Crowell Ridge. Also, the many dips and rises of the trail means you'll probably climb at least double the elevation gain listed.

Getting There

■ From the end of the bridge that spans the Pend Oreille River in Metaline Falls, drive north on Highway 31 for 2.1 miles to Sullivan Lake Road.

■ Turn right and drive 4.6 miles to Forest Service Road 2212 which is marked by a sign which reads "Highline Road" and "Crowell Ridge". Turn left and from here it's 18 miles of gravel road to the trailhead.

■ At 3.4 miles you'll come to a fork in the road. To the left is the Sullivan Lookout Tower Road. If you're a couch potato, drive the eight miles of rocky, bumpy road to within a half mile of the summit. Make sure you have a high-clearance vehicle, too.

■ If you're trail-toughened, bear right, following the sign which reads "Gypsy-Leola Road". At 11.4 miles, you'll reach a T-intersection. Though a sign here says it's eight miles to the end of the road, it's actually 6.6 miles. Follow the sign and drive to the Bear Pasture Trailhead at the end of the road.

■ The entire way is passable by low-clearance vehicle, however the last two miles of road passes through a clear-cut on a very steep slope. The road is narrow and there are numerous bumps and water berms, but it's still passable if you drive carefully.

The Trail
Crowell Ridge Trail #515
Starting elevation: 5,560 feet
Rating: Major Workout
Info: Sullivan Lake Ranger District
USGS topo map: Gypsy Peak

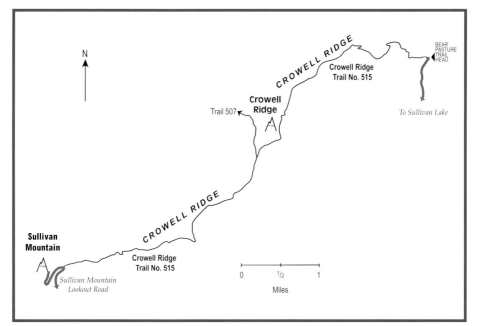

The Crowell Ridge trail begins in a clear-cut before entering the Salmo-Priest Wilderness. You'll huff your way uphill for about 45 minutes until reaching the top of the ridge. The trail turns to the southwest and you'll pass through mostly open country while traversing Crowell Ridge. About three miles into the hike, you may notice the collapsed roof of the old lookout atop the high point of Crowell Ridge. The trail passes well below it, but if you want to climb it, continue past until reaching a trail junction marked by a pair of signs. Leave the trail here and head upslope and in ten minutes you'll be atop Crowell.

Back at the trail junction, follow the sign and resume your hike along Crowell Ridge Trail #515. Soon after this junction, the landscape becomes timbered and stays that way for the rest of the hike.

At several points along the trail, you'll be able to see the lookout tower up ahead at the top of Sullivan Mountain. When you reach the end of the trail, you'll have a half-mile walk up the gated summit road to the top.

From the Summit

Looking west into the valley below you, the towns of Metaline and Metaline Falls are easily visible. Long stretches of the Pend Oreille River to the west and south can also be seen.

Looking west across the Pend Oreille River valley, the higher-elevation mountain about ten miles away with clear-cuts on its lower slopes is Abercrombie Mountain (#2: 7,308 feet). A couple miles to the right of Abercrombie, connected by a ridge is rocky Hooknose Mountain (#4: 7,210 feet).

Looking roughly nine miles to the northwest, the electrical towers marking Boundary Dam on the Pend Oreille River can be seen.

Looking almost due south, the mountain across the valley, about five miles away is Hall Mountain (#39: 6,323 feet). Poking its pointed peak up in the distance, just to the right of Hall, twelve miles away is Molybdenite Mountain (#16: 6,784 feet). And to the right of Molybdenite Mountain, a distant 32 miles away, the prominent, rounded peak is Calispell Mountain (#14: 6,855 feet)

Mount Leona

6,474 Feet

■ Round-Trip Length: **7 miles** ■ Elevation Gain: **2,224 feet** ■ Hiking Time: **4 hours**

This mountain in the northern end of the Kettle Range is a moderate-length day hike that doesn't require any off-trail bushwhacking. Looking westward from the summit, it gives one of the best views of the Curlew Lake valley of all the Kettle peaks.

The lower reaches of the trail passes through a thick forest of large-diameter Engelmann spruce and Douglas fir—a rare sight in the Kettles. Logging has taken out most of the big trees that past forest fires have missed.

Getting There

■ From Kettle Falls, head west on Highway 395 across the Columbia River and turn left onto State Highway 20 after crossing the bridge.

■ Drive 18.4 miles to graveled Albion Hill Road #2030. Turn right and from here the trailhead is just over 12 miles away.

■ Drive 11.7 miles to the end of road 2030. A sign marking the Stickpin Trailhead and Ryan's Cabin Trailhead is here, telling you to turn left Follow the sign and go two-tenths of a mile to a fork.

■ To the right is marked road #920. Ignore it and bear left After another four-tenths of a mile you'll cross a cattle guard. The trailhead is straight ahead, 50 yards beyond the cattle guard at the end of the road.

The Trail

Stick Pin Trail #71, Kettle Crest Trail #13, and Leona Loop Trail.

Starting elevation: 4,250 feet
Rating: Break a Sweat
Info: Colville Ranger District
USGS topo map: Mt. Leona

In its early reaches, the Stick Pin Trail gradually ascends as it follows a stream.

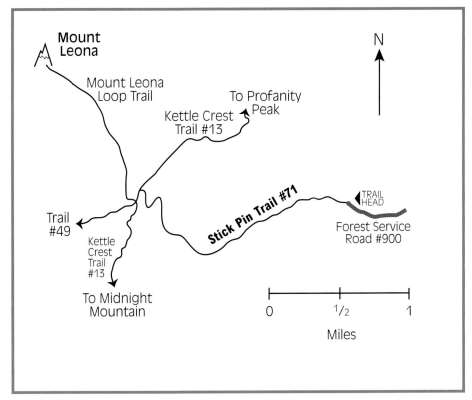

Numerous rough plank bridges and raised earth berms keep you above the wet, boggy areas. Through this section you'll see plenty of large-diameter trees, many of which have toppled because of the soft, wet soil along the streambed.

After about a mile and a quarter, the trail will veer away from the stream and begin a very steep climb up a ravine. This section is short though and the trail soon cuts away from the ravine and returns to a more moderate ascent.

After 2 1/2 miles of hiking, the trail will end when it intersects Kettle Crest Trail #13. Turn left and an additional three or four minutes of walking will bring you to an intersection of three trails. The one on the right is the Leona Loop Trail. A sign mounted on a tree should verify this. Take it, and you'll begin climbing a trail that was built the old-fashioned way—straight and steep.

Though the trail to the summit is supposedly a loop trail, the way down is no longer maintained, so it's actually an out and back trail. As you near the summit, the trail becomes an old jeep road. It's about a mile and a quarter from the Kettle Crest Trail to the summit.

From the Summit

Atop Mt. Leona you'll find a portable trailer that houses a Forest Service transmitting tower.

If you look to the southwest, you'll see an excavation of bare rock on a hillside. This is the Echo Bay open-pit gold mine near Republic.

Looking northeast, about two miles away, the summit of Profanity Peak (#32: 6,423 feet) and its open, south-facing slope can be seen.

Glancing to the southeast, the heavily forested, lower-elevation summit three miles away is U S Mountain (#44: 6,232 feet).

Roundtop Mountain **31**

6,466 Feet

■ Round-Trip Length: **3.2 miles** ■ Elevation Gain: **1,066 feet** ■ Hiking Time: **2 hours**

Here's a peak in the Salmo-Priest Wilderness that's a short, easy day hike. Trailhead to summit shouldn't take more than an hour. However, driving to the trailhead will probably take a good deal longer than the hike.

Though Roundtop Mountain is within a roadless wilderness area, it won't seem like it from the summit. The view is excellent, but you'll find clear-cuts and logging roads in almost every direction you look. The upper reaches of the mountain are within the wilderness area, but much of the lower slopes are not. This is the case with much of the Salmo-Priest Wilderness. It's a carved-up, pared-down wilderness that has had most of the low country cut out for timber production, while the higher country (and its less valuable, smaller trees) is protected. For this reason, you can never go "deep" into the Salmo-Priest Wilderness. No matter where you are, you're always close to a boundary line.

Getting There

■ From the end of the bridge spanning the Pend Oreille River in Metaline Falls, take Highway 31 for 2.1 miles north to Sullivan Lake Road (County Road #9345).
■ Turn right and drive 4.9 miles to graveled Forest Service Road #22 (Ignore Road #2212 which you'll come to first). Road #22 is marked with a sign that lists the mileage to Priest Lake, Salmo Mountain and East Sullivan Campground.
■ Turn left and drive 6.0 miles until coming to a fork. Bear right, staying on Road #22.
■ Drive an additional 8.4 miles, just past the summit of Pass Creek Pass. At the summit there's a sign giving the mileage to Nordman and Priest River, Idaho. Two-tenths of a mile down the other side is a sign pointing out Shedroof Divide Trail #512, and just beyond, a pull-out on the right with parking space for two cars. If the pull-out is full, there's ample parking at the pass summit.

The Trail

Shedroof Divide Trail #512.
Starting Elevation: 5,400 feet
Rating: Break a Sweat
Info: Sullivan Lake Ranger District
USGS topo map: Pass Creek

Round Top Mountain sits adjacent to Pass Creek Pass. As you hike the lower reaches, the summit comes into view from several points along the trail.

The trail climbs the south slope of Round Top Mountain and shortly past the trailhead enters a recently burned area. Catching sight of the summit and its apparently well-groomed, grassy slopes, you'll wonder if someone has been mowing

■ *Roundtop Mountain*

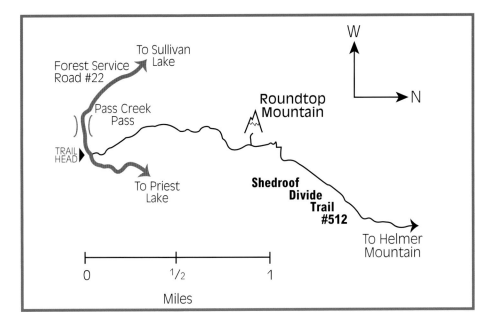

and manicuring the mountainside.

Soon you'll leave the burned area and enter the grassy slopes that you saw earlier. After 30 to 40 minutes of steady uphill hiking, the Shedroof Divide Trail reaches its highest point on Round Top, and this is where you'll find an unmaintained spur trail on the left that leads to the top. Be watchful because a recently fallen tree lies right at this intersection, obscuring the trail. If you start descending, you've missed the trail. Once on the spur trail, the top can be reached within ten minutes

From the Summit

In addition to the old lookout tower that's been knocked down, you'll find that Round Top's grassy and nearly treeless summit is an excellent vantage point, providing unobstructed views.

Looking due west, the peak with the mostly open summit and heavily clear-cut lower slopes six miles distant is Hall Mountain (#39: 6,323 feet). Looking roughly southwest, the pointy peak with the gray, rocky, upper slopes ten miles away is Molybdenite Mountain (#16: 6,784 feet).

Looking northwest, you can just make out the lookout tower atop Sullivan Mountain (#29: 6,483 feet) seven miles away. Just to the left of Sullivan, across the Pend Oreille River valley, 17 miles away, the bare, rocky peaks connected by a ridge are Hooknose Mountain (#4: 7,210 feet) to the right, and Abercrombie Mountain (#2: 7,308 feet) on the left.

To the right of Sullivan Mountain you can see the many knobs that make up Crowell Ridge. Following Crowell Ridge to a high point almost due north, you can see Gypsy Peak (#1: 7,309 feet) ten miles distant.

Looking a little left of northeast, the burned summit, heavily treed with snags and framed in the center of two slopes in the foreground, is Helmer Mountain (#20: 6,734 feet) three miles distant. The peak just to the left of Helmer, a mile closer, also burned, but with a less dense snag cover, is Mankato Mountain (#23: 6,590 feet).

The best view from here though is to the east. The numerous rocky peaks of the Selkirks in north Idaho stretch in a nearly endless line from north to south. Between yourself and the Selkirk Range, beautiful Priest Lake is visible in the valley below.

Profanity Peak

6,423 Feet

■ Round-Trip Length: **7 miles** ■ Elevation Gain: **1,973 feet** ■ Hiking Time: **5 hours**

While climbing this mountain in the Kettle Range, you'll probably get a clear idea what likely inspired its name. Profanity Peak isn't close to being the longest hike, but it rates as one of the toughest. A trail takes you most of the way to the summit, but the upper reaches have to be traversed off-trail. The distance isn't so great, but a profusion of downed trees makes the going slow, tiring, and cumbersome. Your patience and agility may become so taxed, you'll find yourself shouting out profanities.

Though most of the peaks of the Kettle Range are lightly hiked, Profanity may be least hiked of all. There is little evidence of human visitation at the summit. With its mountainous scenery and solitude, you can enjoy a real wilderness outing. And you won't have to worry about being heard as you fill the air with cuss words.

Getting There

■ From Kettle Falls, head west on Highway 395 across the Columbia River and turn left onto State Highway 20 after crossing the bridge.
■ Drive 18.4 miles to graveled Albion Hill Road #2030.
■ Turn right and drive 11.7 miles to the end of Road #2030 where a sign points the way to the Stick Pin and Ryan's Cabin Trailheads. Follow the sign and turn left.
■ At two-tenths of a mile you'll come to a fork. Bear left and drive four-tenths of a mile more to a cattle guard. Turn right immediately after crossing the cattle guard and drive a couple hundred feet to the far end of the loop road.

The Trail

Ryan's Cabin Trail #30 and Kettle Crest Trail #13
Starting elevation: 4,450 feet
Rating: Huffin' & Puffin'
Info: Kettle Falls Ranger District
USGS topo map: Mt. Leona

The Ryan's Cabin trail starts at the far end of the short loop road and is not marked by a sign. It's well-defined though and should be easy to find.

The trail starts in an old clear-cut and passes through it for the first one-half to three-quarters of a mile as it ascends. Shortly after leaving the clear-cut area, you'll pass by the trail's namesake, an old, decrepit cabin slowly being reclaimed by the forest.

About five minutes beyond the cabin, the trail intersects the Kettle Crest Trail. Turn right and follow the Kettle Crest for about 45 minutes of steady uphill hiking through thick forests and dense stands of lodgepole.

When the trail levels out, it's time to leave it by turning right and heading uphill. If you miss your turn-off, the trail immediately leaves the dense stands and turns onto an open, grassy, southwest-facing slope with good views.

There is no trail to the top of Profanity and you'll likely notice the plethora of downed timber in this area, which will make the hike up slow and difficult. The downed trees are like hurdles which must be climbed over, and it doesn't let up until you're nearly at the summit. It's with much relief that after 45 minutes of off-trail walking, you reach the top and are rewarded with a view from the open, south-facing slope.

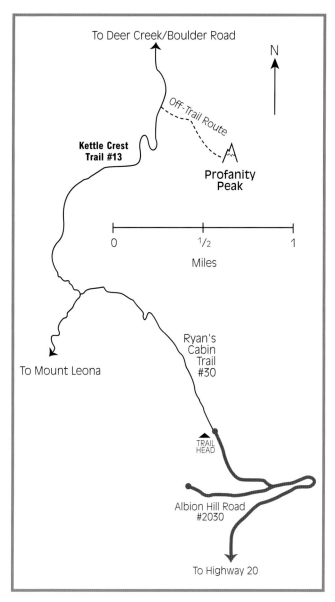

From the Summit

There's no sign or marker at the summit stating you're on Profanity Peak. The only evidence of human visitation you may find is an old rock fire ring.

The summit is well-treed, thus views are limited. However, if you descend the south-facing slope just a little, you'll come to an open bald with great views.

Descending Profanity can be fraught with problems. It's easy to miss the trail and become stranded in the obstacle-strewn forest if you choose to return the way you came up. Probably the best way down is via the open, south-facing slope, heading for the logging road that's visible in the clear-cut below. Using logging roads, you can work your way back to the Ryan's Cabin Trailhead.

Grizzly 33 Mountain

6,397 Feet

■ Round-Trip Length: **7 miles** ■ Elevation Gain: **1,437 feet** ■ Hiking Time: **4 hours**

This beautiful, remote mountain on the Colville Indian Reservation has unusual rock outcroppings at its summit that invite exploration. It's also one of the few peaks on the Top 50 list with a standing lookout tower.

However, it's in an area that's managed primarily for timber production, not recreation. To reach the summit of Grizzly, you'll have to make a long drive over logging roads and through clear-cuts. Be aware that you might happen upon an ongoing logging operation. This is a climb which you'll have to "endure" in the lower reaches until reaching higher elevation.

Getting There

■ From Inchelium High School in Inchelium, drive north on the Inchelium-Kettle Falls Road for 1.2 miles.

■ Turn left onto Hall Creek Road. From here the trailhead is a little over 20 miles away. After a couple miles, Hall Creek Road turns to gravel.

■ At 7.5 miles you'll come to a junction. Hall Creek Road turns left and Elbow Lake Road goes straight, passing a fence line and cattle guard. Bear left, staying on Hall Creek Road.

■ Drive another 4.5 miles until coming to Grizzly Mountain Road. There's a sign marking the road which faces traffic coming the opposite direction. Turn left, immediately crossing a bridge.

■ Ignore a branch road on the right a mile or so into Grizzly Mountain Road until coming to an unmarked fork at 1.9 miles. Here you bear right, and over the next four miles you'll cross three short, steel bridges that span a roadside creek.

■ The road ascends moderately, and at the upper reaches begins passing through clear-cuts. Be sure to ignore a couple branch roads to the right along here until reaching the 9.7 mile mark of Grizzly Mountain Road. At this point you'll be entering another clear-cut and taking a branch road to the right. (Note: If you miss this branch road, you'll reach the high point of Grizzly Mountain Road about three-tenths of a mile later and begin descending into the next valley.)

■ Drive on this branch road for two-tenths of a mile until coming to a Kelly hump blocking the roadway. Park here and begin your hike.

The Trail

Old summit road
Starting Elevation: 4,960 feet
Rating: Huffin' & Puffin'
Info: Colville Tribal Headquarters
USGS topo map: Sitdown Mountain

After crossing the dirt mound blocking the roadway, you'll immediately enter a timber stand, and a couple minutes later, arrive at an intersection of logging roads. Keep going straight, taking the ascending road, and less than ten minutes into your hike, you'll arrive at a clear-cut and be able to see your destination. Grizzly Mountain,

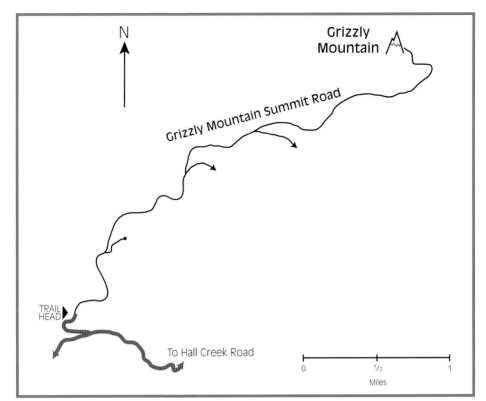

N

Grizzly
Mountain

Grizzly Mountain Summit Road

TRAIL
HEAD

To Hall Creek Road

0   ¹/₂   1
Miles

with its rocky outcrops and fire lookout atop lies straight ahead.

Continue through the clear-cut, avoiding side roads until entering standing timber. About a half hour into the hike, you'll come to a second clear-cut. Follow the road as it descends to the bottom of the clear-cut until arriving at a fork. The main road continues descending, but you'll leave it, taking the rougher branch road that ascends steeply on the left. You'll stay on this road as it soon leaves the clear-cut and takes you to the old, unmaintained summit road.

The first part of the old summit road climbs gently, then soon levels out. In places you can get a glimpse of the lookout tower at the top. But soon the road steepens and the last 3/4 mile is a steep, sweaty climb.

From the Summit

You'll be able to see that the summit consists of a short ridge punctuated by rocky outcroppings in the middle and at each end. Standing near the fire lookout and looking north, you can see that the other end is slightly higher in elevation.

As you look north from the lookout tower, the rock outcropping at the other end evenly splits a ridge in the distance that connects two mountains about 7 miles away. The one on the right is Bald Mountain (#11: 6,940 feet). The one to the left is Edds Mountain (#25: 6,550 feet).

Looking a little to the left of northeast, the broad, rocky, nearly treeless mountain about five miles away is White Mountain (#12: 6,921 feet).

Looking in a southeasterly direction, the mountain with the rocky knob across the valley, 2 to 3 miles distant, is Lynx Mountain at 5,709 feet

And nearly due west, the higher elevation, rounded mountain, about 25 miles away is Moses Mountain (#18: 6,774 feet).

Oregon Butte 34

6,387 Feet
■ Round-Trip Length: **6 miles** ■ Elevation Gain: **887 feet** ■ Hiking Time: **4 hours**
(Northwest Forest Pass required)

The highest peak in the Blue Mountains, Oregon Butte lies in the Wenaha-Tucannon Wilderness Area. It's topped by a picturesque lookout cabin built in 1931 that's listed on the Historic National Register.

Hiking this area is a special pleasure because it lacks the ugly, logged-off landscapes common to other forests. Of course, there's no logging allowed in the wilderness area, but the surrounding Umatilla National Forest hasn't been logged as thoroughly as forests in the northern half of the state. With an extensive trail system, and plenty of open spaces among the rocky ridgetops and basaltic slopes, great views come your way often. This is prime hiking country that is under-used and little-known.

Getting There

■ From Dayton, Washington, the trailhead is a 33-mile drive over mostly gravel roads.

■ Turn off Highway 12 onto 4th Street (a brown sign reading "Ski" points the way for eastbound traffic) and follow the paved highway south out of town for five miles to graveled Hatley Gulch Road.

■ Turn left and make the long uphill climb to a plateau of wheatland. At 9.5 miles you'll reach an unmarked 3-way intersection. Bear right.

■ At 15.4 miles you'll come to another 3-way intersection, in the middle of which sits a rock cairn. Follow the sign

and turn right onto Forest Service Road #46. About a mile beyond the intersection you'll cross a cattleguard and enter the Umatilla National Forest.

■ At 27.0 miles, Road 4608, marked by a sign, intersects on the left. Take it, passing Godwin Guard Station just beyond the intersection.

■ At 30.5 miles, the road splits 3 ways. Bear right and drive to Teepee Trailhead at the end of the road.

The Trail
Mt. Misery Trail #3113
Starting Elevation: 5,500 feet
Rating: Break a Sweat
Info: Pomeroy Ranger Station
USGS topo map: Oregon Butte

Two trails originate at Teepee Trailhead—take the one that has Oregon Butte listed on the trailhead mileage sign.

The trail begins by ascending a heavily wooded north-facing slope. After 20 to 30 minutes of hiking, you'll come to a fork

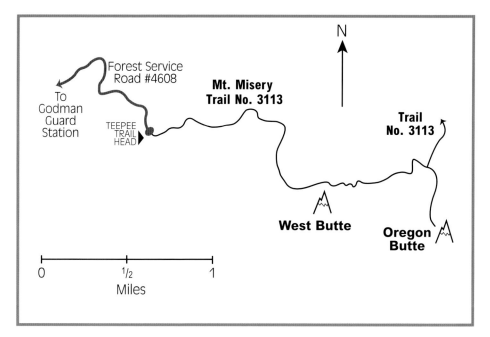

with no sign indicating which trail to take. However, it doesn't matter because the two trails rejoin about a half mile ahead. At this spot, if you're tall enough, you can look above the trees to the west and just see the lookout cabin atop Oregon Butte.

If you take the right branch you'll be traversing the ridge that leads to the summit of West Butte (#40: 6,292 feet). If you desire, a very short off-trail diversion will take you to the top.

From the point where the two trails rejoin, you'll descend into the saddle between West Butte and Oregon Butte. After bottoming out, you'll begin scaling Oregon Butte's west slope. Thirty minutes of climbing will bring you to the crest of another ridge, and you'll see the trail descending steeply down the other side. Don't take it, follow the branch trail on the right that goes up the slightly ascending ridgeline. In less than ten minutes you'll reach the summit and lookout cabin atop Oregon Butte.

From the Summit

Depending on availability of willing personnel, the lookout cabin may or may not be staffed. If staffed, plan on spending a little time chatting as the lookouts generally welcome visitors to their isolated summer abode. Don't ask for food or drink since everything has to be carried in. In fact, bringing some fresh fruit, produce, or other perishable would be a welcome surprise for the lookout personnel.

Looking a little to the left of due south, the snowcapped Wallowa Mountains in Oregon can be seen, 50 to 60 miles away. To the left of them, roughly southeast, eighty miles distant, the jagged peaks of the Seven Devils Range in Idaho are visible.

Across the valley to the west, about a mile away is West Butte (#40: 6,292 feet) which you traversed to get here. Looking in the opposite direction, the two high points rising 7 to 8 miles away in the east are Diamond Peak (#36: 6,379 feet) to the left and Mt. Misery (#37: 6,366 feet) to the right.

Looking roughly southwest, the ski runs of Bluewood Ski Area are visible about 8 miles away.

Leola Peak

6,380 Feet

■ Round-Trip Length: **10 miles** ■ Elevation Gain: **820 feet** ■ Hiking Time: **8 hours**

An entire summer may pass without a single visitor to this mountain that sits just outside the Salmo-Priest Wilderness. Because it's overshadowed by higher, more prominent peaks nearby, and there's no trail leading to the summit, few people wander this peak's way. If you're looking for solitude and a demanding backcountry hike, choose Leola Peak.

The route to Leola is mostly off-trail, and it's a fairly long hike with some bush-whacking required. Add in the long drive from Sullivan Lake and you've got what could be the most remote mountain on the Top 50 list.

On your way to Leola you'll brush past the highest peak on the list, Gypsy Peak, which is a two- to three-hour sidetrip. If you get an early start, and you're hiking in the long daylight period of early summer, you can scale both Gypsy and Leola in one day.

Also, keep in mind the elevation gain is several hundred feet more than the difference between trailhead and peak.

Getting There

■ From the end of the bridge that spans the Pend Oreille River in Metaline Falls, take Highway 31 north for 2.1 miles to Sullivan Lake Road (County Road 9345).
■ Turn right and drive 4.6 miles to graveled Forest Service Road No. 2212 where a sign points the way to Crowell Ridge and the Highline Road. Turn left and from here it's about 18 miles to the Bear Pasture Trailhead.
■ At 3.4 miles, there's a fork, follow the sign and bear right, taking the Gypsy-Leola Road.
■ At 11.4 miles you'll come to a T-intersection. Follow the sign, turning left onto Crowell Ridge Road and drive to the end

of the road. The sign says it's 8 miles away, but it's actually 6.6 miles.
■ The road is well maintained except for the last two miles as it traverses a clear-cut on a steep hillside. Though passable by low-clearance car, the going is very slow due to the numerous dips, bumps, and water berms.
■ You'll notice a sign and gate just after turning onto Crowell Ridge Road. This is where the road to Bear Pasture Trailhead is closed on August 15th each year for wildlife considerations.

The Trail

Crowell Ridge Trail #515
Starting elevation: 5,560 feet
Info: Sullivan Lake Ranger District
Rating: Major Workout
USGS topo map: Salmo Peak

You'll travel by trail at the start of this hike, but most of it will be off-trail along open, rocky ridgelines where the going is easy. But the last mile as you approach summit is toughest as you'll have to bush-whack through chest-high brush.

Leaving the trailhead at Bear Pasture, take the Crowell Ridge Trail toward Sullivan Mountain. This trail takes you through an old clear-cut until passing into the Salmo-Priest Wilderness Area. The trail climbs until reaching Cowell Ridge, about 45 minutes into the hike. The trail levels out at the ridgetop and turns southwest, heading toward Sullivan Mountain. At this point you'll turn right, leaving the trail and following the ridge in a northerly direction.

You'll have some steep slopes to negotiate as the ridge rises and falls. About an hour after leaving the trail, you'll come to

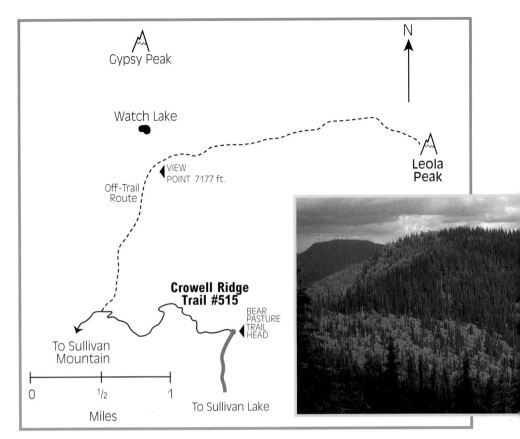

a high point and see Watch Lake in the plunging valley below you. Looking north, directly across the valley a mile or so away is Gypsy Peak, at 7,309 feet, the highest point in Eastern Washington.

As you face north, look to the right and see the descending ridge heading east. The ridge bottoms out, then rises in the distance, connecting to Leola, which is the timbered peak 2-3 miles distant. It has three large rectangular clear-cuts in a row on its lower slopes.

Follow the ridge all the way to the summit of Leola. From the ridge high point overlooking Watch Lake, it's about a two-hour hike.

From the Summit

At the top of Leola you'll find a rock cairn which supports a USGS cadastral survey marker. It marks the boundary between Forest Service land and the Salmo-Priest Wilderness Area.

Looking down into the valley on the east side of Leola, you can see Road 2220 switchbacking its way up to Salmo Mountain (#15: 6,828 feet) which is nearly due north, about 2 1/2 miles away. The lookout tower at the summit is easy to see.

Looking due east, Shedroof Mountain (#19: 6,764 feet) is plainly visible across the valley, three miles distant.

Looking northeast, the taller mountain, 7 to 8 miles distant, that consists of three separate peaks grouped closely together is Snowy Top Mountain (7,572 feet) in Idaho. It sits a mere half mile from the Canadian border.

Looking west from where you came, Gypsy Peak is obvious, a little to the right of due west, about two miles distant. The next highest point on the ridge running north from Gypsy Peak is South Fork (#5: 7,152 feet), which lies almost due northwest.

6,379 Feet
■ Round-Trip Length: **2 miles** ■ Elevation Gain: **499 feet** ■ Hiking Time: **1 hr.**
(Northwest Forest Pass required)

One of three mountains on the Top 50 list in the Wenaha-Tucannon Wilderness Area, Diamond Peak is a short, easy climb, as the trailhead parking lot sits at the edge of the wilderness boundary, barely a quarter mile from the summit.

Though easily accessed by car, this peak, as well as others in the Blue Mountains, is far from major highways, reachable only by a long drive over dusty, gravel roads. This remoteness means you'll probably encounter only an occasional backpacker or horseman, if anyone. Avoid the high-use period in the fall when hunters swarm into the Blues.

Sitting little more than a mile from Diamond Peak is No. 37 Mount Misery. Its proximity, and the fairly short gain in elevation, makes climbing both mountains quick and easy.

Getting There

■ While driving west on Highway 12 through Pomeroy, turn left onto 15th Street, marked by a brown sign which reads, "Umatilla National Forest 15 miles." From here it's just over 37 miles to the trailhead.

■ 15th Street heads south out of town and ascends continuously past fields of wheat for a little over 15 miles before crossing a cattle guard where a sign announces you're entering the Umatilla National Forest. Here the road turns to gravel.

■ Avoid turnoffs until the 32.5 mile mark where a large yellow sign warns the way ahead narrows to a single-lane dirt road. A few feet beyond this sign turn right onto Road 4030.

■ Right away you'll see another sign reading "Mt. Misery Trail #3113: 5 miles." Barely a tenth of a mile beyond, the road forks. Bear right and drive to the trailhead at the end of the road.

The Trail

Mt. Misery Trail #3113
Starting elevation: 5,880 feet
Rating: Easy
Info: Pomeroy Ranger Station
USGS topo map: Diamond Peak

A sign at the trailhead states you're entering the Wenaha-Tucannon Wilderness and that Diamond Peak is one mile away. If you ignored the trail and climbed the steep

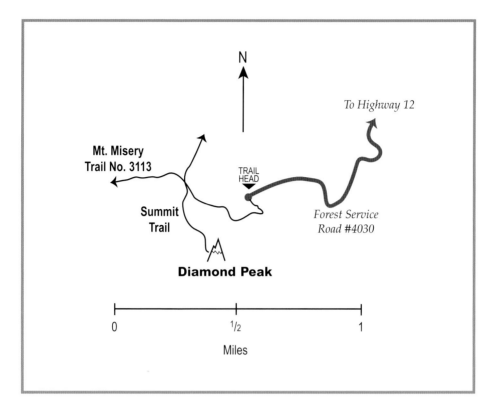

slope westward from the trailhead, the hike would be much shorter. However, it's assumed you'll take the trail.

The trail begins climbing right away and you'll pass through a lush, north-facing slope until coming to a trail intersection at an open bald about 25 minutes into your hike. Here you'll find a pair of signs only a few feet apart. One points out Trail 3110 which heads north to the Tucannon River, and the other warns the trail is closed to motor vehicles.

According to maps, the summit trail to Diamond intersects on the left here, but it's no longer maintained and cannot be seen. However, if you backtrack about 60-70 feet from the trail intersection, then leave the trail and walk southward a short distance through the open meadow into the timber stand, the trail can be found among the trees. Even if you can't find the trail, continue uphill and in a few minutes you'll arrive at the open ridge that leads to the summit. After leaving Mt. Misery Trail, the summit is only about a ten-minute hike.

From the Summit
Atop the summit you'll find a Forest Service radio tower and a USGS marker indentifying the peak.

Looking just to the left of due south, the snowcapped Wallowa Mountains can be seen in Oregon, about 60 miles away. Looking roughly southeast, another rocky, craggy range even further in the distance is the Seven Devils Mountains in Idaho.

Looking eastward, the neighboring peak, little more than a mile away is Misery Mountain (#37- 6,366 feet). Looking nearly due west, Oregon Butte (#34: 6,387 feet) is easily visible, though hard to pick out among all the ridgelines. It's the highest point in the Blues, about seven miles from where you stand.

37 Mount Misery

6,366 Feet

Round-Trip Length: **2 miles** ▪ Elevation Gain: **436 feet** ▪ Hiking Time: **1 hr.**
(Northwest Forest Pass required)

An open knob rising gently above the surrounding ridges and bluffs deep in the Blue Mountains, Mt. Misery is an unspectacular peak that gives spectacular vistas of the Blues, of rocky, snow-capped ranges that rise afar, and mile after mile of forest and rolling farmland in between.

A well-maintained Forest Service road passes close to the summit, allowing a short twenty-minute hike to the top, far shorter than the 34-mile drive out of Pomeroy, much of it over dusty, graveled roads.

This hike can be easily combined with an ascent of #36 Diamond Peak nearby.

Getting There
▪ Mt. Misery is accessed using the same route as #36 Diamond Peak. While driving west through Pomeroy on Highway 12, turn left on 15th Street where a sign reads, "Umatilla National Forest 15 miles". Stay on this road as it ascends past mile after mile of wheat fields until crossing a cattleguard and entering the national forest.

▪ The paved road turns to gravel and you'll stay on it, avoiding numerous turn-offs until the 32.5 mile mark where a large yellow sign warns the road ahead turns to a single-wide dirt lane. Just a few yards past this sign turn right onto Road 4030.

▪ Right away you'll see a sign stating that Mt. Misery Trail #3113 is five miles distant, which is further than you need to go. Just beyond this sign you'll come to a fork at which you'll bear right.

▪ Eight-tenths of a mile into Road 4030, you'll come around a corner to a good view of Mt. Misery, its twin-humped summit barely a mile away, if that. The ravine that separates the two humps descends to the road, and that's where you'll start your hike, 1.7 miles into Road 4030, at a place called Kelly Camp.

▪ Situated next to a wide spot in the road where it turns sharply north, you'll need good eyes to see a weathered sign that reads, "Kelly Camp" nailed to a tall tamarack. Park here and look for the trail on the left-hand side of the road.

The Trail
Mt. Misery Trail #3113
Starting Elevation: 5,930 feet
Rating: Easy
Info: Pomeroy Ranger Station
USGS topo map: Diamond Peak

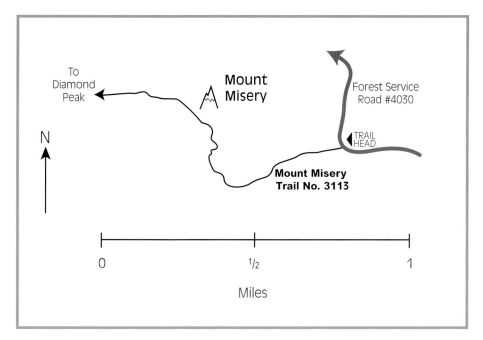

From Kelly Camp, Mt. Misery Trail heads west from the left side of the road. There is no trailhead sign, nor is there an obvious trail in the road embankment save a row of rocks outlining the trail entrance. Search around for it and you'll find the path obvious and easy to follow just beyond the road.

The trail climbs for about 10 minutes through an old clear-cut before leveling out as it reaches a timbered stretch, followed by a meadow. Here the trail is very near the summit, but skirts it before descending as it heads to Diamond Peak. Turn right off the trail here, about 15 minutes into your hike, and walk up the open south-facing slope to the summit, a three- or four-minute off-trail walk.

From the Summit

The summit is an open, rocky meadow with no sign or marker indicating you're at the top of Mt. Misery.

Almost due south, about 60 miles away, the snow-capped Wallowa Mountains in Oregon are easily seen. Looking roughly southeast, a rocky, craggy collection of peaks, visible even further in the distance are the Seven Devil Range in Idaho.

Less than a quarter mile away, just to the left of due south, the other half of Misery's twin humps juts upward. Though it may look higher, according to USGS maps, it's 34 feet lower in elevation than your vantage point.

If you can look past the trees to the west, the next-door mountain, little more than a mile away, is Diamond Peak (#36: 6,379 feet). It's heavily forested on its north-facing side, while its south-facing side is bare and mostly open.

From your vantage point you'll see that the Blue Mountains have a different look than the protruding, uplifted rock masses that give the Cascades or Wallowas their stark, forbidding appearance. The Blues are characterized by relatively flat peaks surrounded by deep, plunging ravines. This was caused by repeated lava flows over millions of years that built the landscape up, layer by layer. Over time, erosion cut the channels and ravines you see now, leaving the uneroded parts as "mountaintops."

38

Sherlock Peak

6,365 Feet

■ Round-Trip Length: **4 miles** ■ Elevation Gain: **1,965 feet** ■ Hiking Time: **2 hours**

Sherlock Peak is a lightly hiked, yet fairly short and easy peak to conquer. It lies northeast of Colville, in the same vicinity as Mt. Abercrombie and Mt. Linton.

A recently constructed trail makes a gentle climb to the summit compared to the old trail which went nearly straight up. At the top you'll find several nearby peaks that are connected by a system of ridgelines. You may want to give yourself some extra time for a little off-trail exploring.

Getting There

■ While traveling north through Colville on Main Street (Highway 395), turn right onto Third Street (Highway 20) and go 1.2 miles to the top of the hill.
■ Turn left onto Aladdin Road and drive 25.4 miles until reaching a Y in the road. Bear right and drive 7.3 miles, going past Deep Lake until reaching Silver Creek Road.
■ Turn right onto this graveled road, and from here it's 8.8 miles to the trailhead.
■ At .6 miles, the road forks. Bear left. At 1.5 miles the road crosses a cattle guard and becomes Forest Service Road 7078.
■ At 1.9 miles the road forks again. Bear right onto Forest Service Road 070.
■ At 2.4 miles turn right onto marked Forest Service Road 075. It's easy to miss the road and the marker among the tall weeds, so keep your eyes peeled.
■ Road 075 immediately descends and crosses Silver Creek via a wooden bridge before beginning a long uphill climb. This road is passable by passenger cars, but

has numerous rocky stretches that make the going slow.
■ At 7.1 miles, you'll come to a three-way fork. If you're driving a low-clearance car you'll have to park and walk the mile and a half to the trailhead. Take the fork with the boulders littering the roadway that heads steeply uphill. If you have a high-clearance vehicle and can get past the boulders, the road gets better beyond it.

The Trail
Mt. Sherlock Trail No.139
Starting elevation: 4,400 feet
Rating: Break a Sweat
Info: Colville Ranger District
USGS topo map: Deep Lake

The trail information above does not include the mile-and-a-half hike from the three-way intersection to the trailhead at the end of Road #075 where you'll find a sign and trail register.

The trail begins by switchbacking up a forested slope before breaking out on Sherlock's open upper slopes. The mountain comes into view here, and soon after you'll pass by a spring where you can see the steeply ascending old trail.

As the peak is approached, the trail levels out when it reaches the saddle

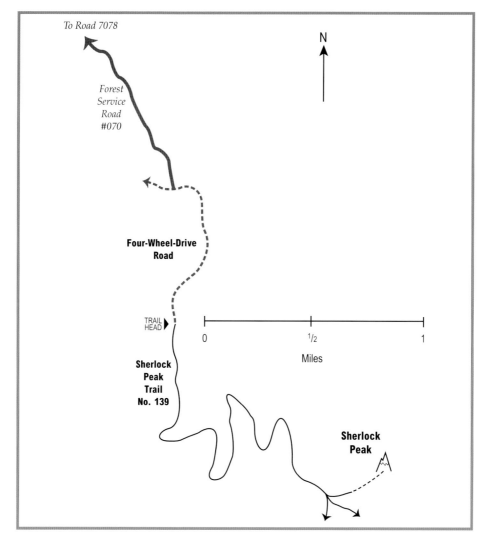

between Sherlock and a peak to the west, and here you'll find the trail branches three ways. Take the least maintained one to the left. This trail soon disappears, but the rocky butte that marks the summit is less than a half mile ahead, and the walking is easy through the open, grassy ridgeline.

From the Summit

Looking roughly northeast from the summit, you'll see the tallest peak in the vicinity, Mt. Abercrombie (#2: 7,308 feet) about five miles away.

You'll have great views of the Deep Lake valley lying to the west, and the Canadian Selkirk Mountains to the north.

Looking due east, rocky-topped Mt. Linton (#45: 6,215 feet) sits three miles away. It's possible to combine this hike with an ascent of Linton if you don't mind a little bushwhacking. Return to the saddle where the trail splits into three and take the middle trail. Though this unmaintained trail comes and goes, it's decipherable most of the time and takes you around the backside of Sherlock and along the ridge that connects to Mt. Linton.

Hall Mountain

6,323 Feet

■ Round-Trip Length: **5 miles** ■ Elevation Gain: **1,003 feet** ■ Hiking Time: **4 hours**

Hall Mountain rises high above Sullivan Lake near Metaline Falls. It's a popular area for day hikes with three separate trailheads that give access to the summit. Hall Mountain is also known for the bighorn sheep that inhabit its rocky slopes.

Being near the Salmo-Priest Wilderness and grizzly bear habitat, the hike described here is open only from July 1st through August 14th each summer. Forest Service Road #500 leading to the trailhead is closed to permit an environment free of motorized vehicles for bears as they search the higher reaches for huckleberries. However, the trail itself is always open. After August 15th, Hall Mountain can still be accessed from the more distant trailheads at Pass Creek Pass and Noisy Creek Campground.

Getting There

■ From the end of the bridge spanning the Pend Oreille River in Metaline Falls, drive north on Highway 31 for 2.1 miles.
■ Turn right onto Sullivan Lake Road (County Road #9345) and drive 4.9 miles to Forest Service Road #22 (Don't confuse this with Road #2212 which you'll come to first).

■ Turn left onto Road #22 and after a quarter mile of pavement, the road turns to gravel. Drive another three miles to reach Forest Service Road #500. Turn right, immediately crossing Sullivan Creek over a paved bridge.

■ Road #500 ascends continuously for 7.3 miles until reaching the trailhead at the end of the road.

The Trail

Hall Mountain Trail #540
Starting elevation: 5,320 feet
Rating: Break a Sweat
Info: Sullivan Lake Ranger District
USGS map: Metaline Falls

At the end of Road 500, thick-growing alders obscure the trailhead sign. Begin your hike by heading uphill, and you'll find the trailhead sign just beyond the parking area.

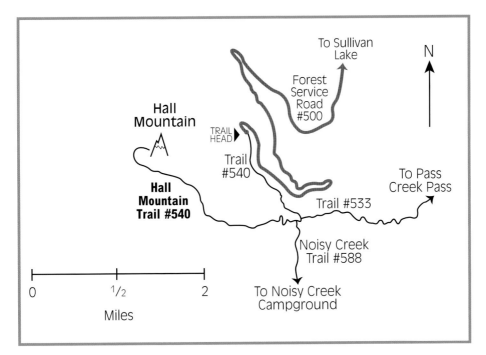

The first mile of the trail is an old logging road which gently ascends Hall's northeast slope. After 20 minutes of steady walking, the road narrows to a path, and you'll reach the intersection with Trail 533 which provides access from Pass Creek Pass. Walk another 20 to 30 yards and you'll reach the intersection of Trail 588 from Noisy Creek Campground. From this point, the Hall Mountain Trail steepens and narrows.

The trail switchbacks a couple times before rising above the timbered slopes to the open and grassy upper slopes. A profusion of wildflowers graces these slopes by mid-July.

The trail runs westward as it climbs at a moderate angle, and through this section the views to the south and west are excellent. The last 50 yards are steepest as the trail climbs to the summit on the west-facing slope.

From the Summit

As with many mountains on the Top 50 list, Hall Mountain has the remains of an old fire lookout laying in a heap on its summit.

As you face westward, the south end of Sullivan Lake is visible, more than 3,500 feet below at the base of the mountain. Looking nearly due north, the peak with the lookout tower about five miles distant is Sullivan Mountain (#29: 6,483 feet).

Looking due east, the rounded knob rising from the ridgeline, with the heavily clear-cut west-facing slope six miles away, is Roundtop Mountain (#31: 6,466 feet). Looking beyond Roundtop, the rocky Selkirk Mountain Range is easy to see in North Idaho.

Looking across the Pend Oreille River valley toward the northwest, the two rocky, prominent peaks connected by a ridge 12 miles away are Hooknose Mountain (#4: 7,210 feet) to the right and Abercrombie Mountain (#2: 7,308 feet) to the left

Looking west, if the day is clear, you can see the Kettle Crest Range in the distance. If you've done a lot of hiking in the Kettles, you can pick out individual peaks from the top of Hall Mountain.

West Butte

6,292 Feet

■ Round-Trip Length: **4 miles** ■ Elevation Gain: **792 feet** ■ Hiking Time: **2 hours**
(Northwest Forest Pass required)

Of the highest 50 peaks in Eastern Washington, West Butte is one of 13 that lie within or on the boundary line of a wilderness area.

Located in the Blue Mountains of southeastern Washington, West Butte is a seldom visited, but easy-to-reach peak that gives an excellent view of the rocky, plunging ravines that characterize the Blues. From the summit, one can also see distant ranges in Oregon and Idaho.

West Butte sits barely a mile by trail from Oregon Butte, the highest point in the Blue Mountains. Both peaks are reached from the same trailhead and can be easily climbed in one day.

Getting There

The trailhead for this hike is the same as #34 Oregon Butte. From Dayton it's a 33-mile drive almost entirely over well-maintained gravel roads.

From Highway 12, turn south onto 4th Street where a sign reading "Ski" points the way. Drive five miles until coming to Hatley Gulch Road.

Turn left onto this gravel road and make the long uphill climb to a plateau of wheatland. You'll come to an unmarked three-way intersection at 9.5 miles. Bear right and continue to the 15.4-mile mark and another three-way intersection in the middle of which sits a rock cairn.

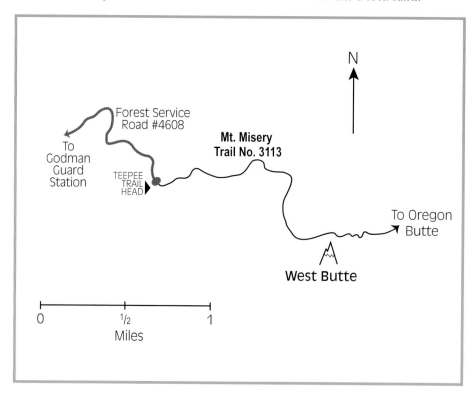

Follow the sign and turn right onto Forest Service Road # 46. A mile beyond this intersection you'll cross a cattle-guard and enter the Umatilla National Forest.

Follow Road 46 to the 27-mile mark where a sign points out Road 4608. Turn left onto this road, passing Godwin Ranger Station just beyond the intersection. At 30.5 miles you'll come to a three-way fork. Bear right and drive to Teepee Trailhead at the end of the road.

The Trail

Mt. Misery Trail #3113
Starting elevation: 5,500 feet
Rating: Break a Sweat
Info: Pomeroy Ranger Statio
USGS topo map: Oregon Butte

From Teepee Trail-head, Trail 3113 heads west into the Wenaha-Tucannon Wilderness Area as it ascends West Butte's west-facing slope. About a half hour into the hike you'll come to an un-marked fork. The two trails rejoin after a half mile, but to reach West Butte's summit, you'll need to bear right.

The trail soon comes to the broad and open West Butte Ridge where you'll have great views to the south. The trail climbs the ridge until veering to the left just short of the summit. Turn right and walk uphill, leaving the trail where a downed tree has left a large hole in the middle of the path. In less than a minute, you'll reach the summit of West Butte.

From the Summit

There's a USGS marker atop West Butte labeled "Oreon Butte," an incorrect placement and spelling for nearby Oregon Butte, the peak less than a mile to the west with the lookout cabin atop.

Looking just to the left of due south, the snow-capped Wallowa Mountains in Oregon are visible 60 miles away. Roughly southeast, another jagged range of mountains is visible even further in the distance. They are the Seven Devils range in Idaho.

Looking southwest, the mountainside clear-cuts about five miles away are the ski runs of Bluewood Ski area.

Prouty Peak

6,263 Feet
■ Round-Trip Length: **6 miles** ■ Elevation Gain: **703 feet** ■ Hiking Time: **5 hours**

This remote mountain near the Salmo-Priest Wilderness Area is a challenge to climb. There's no maintained trail, and in places, thick, chest-high brush blocks the route.

However, the Civilian Conservation Corps constructed a lookout tower and cabin here in the 1930s. The trail that serviced the lookout tower, though unmaintained for decades, can still be found in places. This eases the climb somewhat.

Similar to Leola Peak, which lies a couple miles to the north, both mountains require difficult, off-trail excursions, and are overshadowed by higher-elevation peaks nearby which have easier access. Thus, human visitors are rare, and bagging Prouty gives you membership in a very exclusive club.

Keep in mind that access to the trailhead is limited by closure of the last 6.6 miles of the road on August 15th of each year.

Getting There

■ From the end of the bridge that spans the Pend Oreille River in Metaline Falls, drive 2.1 miles north on Highway 31 to Sullivan Lake Road (County Road #9345).
■ Turn right and drive 4.6 miles to graveled Forest Service Road #2212 which is marked by a sign pointing the way to Crowell Ridge and Highline Road. Turn left and from here it is 18 miles of gravel road to the trailhead at Bear Pasture.
■ At 3.4 miles the road forks. Bear right onto Gypsy-Leola Road.
■ At 11.4 miles you'll come to a T-intersection. A sign here points the way to the end of the road 8 miles distant. Turn left

and drive to the end which is actually 6.6 miles away. Note also the gate and sign that mentions the road closure on August 15th.

■ Road #2212 is a well-maintained gravel road save the last two miles which must be negotiated slowly because of the narrow, rocky roadway and the numerous water berms.

The Trail
No maintained trail
Starting elevation: 5,560 feet
Rating: Huffin' & Puffin'
Info: Sullivan Lake Ranger District
USGS topo map: Salmo Mountain

Arriving at Bear Pasture Trailhead at the end of the road, you'll find a sign pointing out the Crowell Ridge Trail to Sullivan Mountain. You'll go in the opposite direction to reach Prouty Peak however. Just follow the slightly ascending ridge that heads southeast from the parking lot. Your way looks like tough going through thick undergrowth, but once you start, you should find a trail right away. Look for colored plastic blazes.

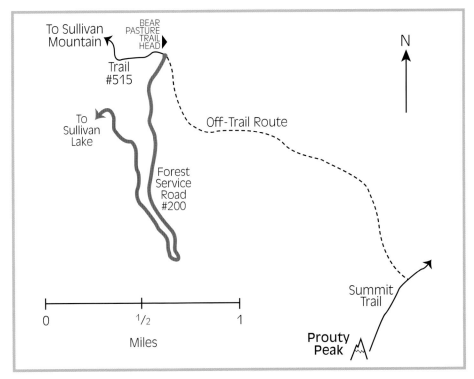

The first mile or so the trail disappears and reappears numerous times. You'll have to do a lot of bushwhacking, but about a half hour into your hike the trail will finally become visible enough to follow consistently. It follows the crest of the ridge until coming to some steep rises where it will veer to the right, bypassing the ridge crest. As you come to some open areas, you'll be able to see Prouty ahead of you. The summit is ridge-like, with a high point at each end, the one on the right (south end) being the highest.

An hour and a half into your hike, the old trail will connect with the distinct summit trail. Turn right and it'll lead you to the top in about ten minutes.

From the Summit

Just south of the high point of Prouty, you'll find an open area where the remains of the old lookout tower and cabin. Looking west across the valley, the crest of Crowell Ridge is easy to see, 2 or 3 miles away.

Looking a bit right of due east, the mountain across the valley, two and a half miles away with the double, rounded humps, is Thunder Mountain. (#24: 6,560 feet). Following the ridgeline south from Thunder, the next mountain, with the burned summit and two open, rocky patches on its north slope, is Helmer Mountain. (#20: 6,734 feet).

Looking a little right of due south, the pointed peak 15 miles distant with the rocky slopes is Molybdenite Mountain (#16: 6,784 feet).

If you can see past the trees, the mountain across the valley to the southwest with clear-cuts on its lower slopes about 9 miles away is Hall Mountain (#39: 6,323 feet).

There's another old, unmaintained trail which leads to Prouty Peak east from Gypsy Meadows. This trail is in better shape than the trail from Bear Pasture. But because of its length, along with numerous blowdowns, it's a more difficult route.

Grassy Top Mountain

6,253 Feet
■ Round-Trip Length: **8 miles** ■ Elevation Gain: **893 feet** ■ Hiking Time: **5 hours**

Lying just south of the Salmo-Priest Wilderness, Grassy Top Mountain can be reached by a well-maintained trail that passes through uncut forest from trailhead to summit.

More of a ridge than a single-peaked mountain, the summit of Grassy Top is actually the lowest of three peaks along the ridge. If you're the adventurous sort, hiking along the ridge instead of the trail on your return will take you to the higher peaks.

A popular trail for hikers and bicyclists, and a National Recreation Trail as well, this hike is still relatively uncrowded. Bring along a container if you hike Grassy Top in August, there are plenty of huckleberries along the way.

Getting There
■ From the end of the bridge that spans the Pend Oreille River in Metaline Falls, drive 2.1 miles north on Highway 31 to Sullivan Lake Road (County Road 9345).

■ Turn right and drive 4.9 miles to Forest Service Road #22 (Note: Ignore Road #2212 at 4.6 miles) marked by a sign listing the mileage to Priest Lake, Salmo Peak, and East Sullivan Campground. Turn left and from here the trailhead is just over 14 miles of well-maintained gravel.

■ Six miles into Road 22 you'll come to a three-way intersection. Bear right, staying on Road #22.

■ Drive an additional 8.1 uphill miles toward Pass Creek Pass until coming to the trailhead sign at the side of the road. There's parking for a couple cars next to the sign. Additional parking is a tenth of a mile ahead at the summit of Pass Creek Pass.

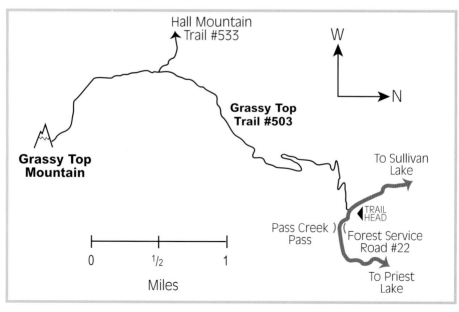

The Trail

Trail No. 503
Starting Elevation: 5,360 Feet
Rating: Break a Sweat
Info: Sullivan Lake Ranger District
USGS topo map: Pass Creek Pass

Trail 503 cuts through a thickly-wooded hillside and begins switchbacking as it climbs upward. But the trail ascends at a moderate rate, and after about 45 minutes of hiking, the trail levels out as it reaches and follows a ridge crest. About an hour and a half into the hike you'll arrive at a trail intersection and find Trail 533 to Hall Mountain. Ignore this and continue on Trail 503 for another 1.1 miles to Grassy Top.

The trail is level as it cuts through an open, grassy slope for most of the final mile. You'll begin climbing again as you re-enter a timber stand, and upon exiting the stand you'll find yourself arriving at the summit of Grassy Top Mountain.

From the Summit

There's no sign or marker to let you know you've reached the top. The summit is flat, grassy, and surrounded by a ring of small trees around the edge. If you continue past the summit, the trail will widen to a four-wheel-drive road and begin descending.

Looking eastward, you'll have a great view of the north Idaho Selkirk Range. To the northeast, 5 to 6 miles away, the two burned summits sitting barely a mile apart, covered with gray snags are Helmer Mountain (#20: 6,734 feet) to the right, and Mankato Mountain (#23: 6,590 feet) to the left Looking just left of these peaks, the open, grassy summit only three miles away is Round Top Mountain (#31: 6,466 feet).

Looking nearly due north, the high point 13 miles distant is Gypsy Peak (#1: 7,309 feet).

If you can find a spot that allows an unencumbered view to the southeast, Priest Lake is visible in the distant valley below.

If you'd like to climb one of the higher points of Grassy Top, take the unmaintained trail that branches to the left as you approached the summit. Though hard to distinguish in places, it takes you back to the intersection with Trail 533 along the ridgetop.

Table Rock

6,250 Feet
Round-Trip Length: **1 mile** ■ Elevation Gain: **203 feet** ■ Hiking Time: **1 hr.**

A distinctive, prominent landmark deep in the Blue Mountains, Table Rock and several other like-named peaks scattered throughout the Northwest earned their names because of the same feature. All have long, flat summits and steep sides which resemble a giant table.

This peak is the only one on the Top 50 list where it's almost certain you'll find a manned fire lookout in summer. The drainage that supplies Walla Walla with its water lies here, thus the need for quick response in case of fire.

Since the lookout tower has road access, the summit can be reached without taking a step outside your car. This hike, however, assumes you'll walk the short summit road.

Getting There

■ From Highway 12 in Dayton, turn south onto 4th Street where a sign reading "Ski" points the way. From here the trailhead is just over 30 miles away.

■ Take 4th Street out of town, following the signs to Bluewood Ski Area. At about 14 miles, the road changes to gravel; at 21.1 you'll pass the ski area turnoff. A sign here warns the road ahead is single-lane with turn-outs. It's not so narrow, however, and the roadway is graveled and well-maintained.

■ The road does climb more steeply though, and at 24 miles you'll intersect with Forest Service Road #46. Don't turn, but continue on another three-tenths of a mile to Road #64. A sign marks the road and on the signpost is a confusing marker with an arrow that reads "Griffith Peak". Turn left onto Road 64, which doesn't lead to Griffith Peak, and just past the intersection you'll come to a mileage sign showing Table Rock is five miles distant.

■ Road 64 is very rough, bumpy, and rocky. Though traverseable by low-clearance vehicle, it's slow going. It'll take about half an hour to drive the five miles. Four miles into Road 64, you'll come around a corner to a good view of Table Rock and the lookout tower. At the marked summit road, park your car at the roadside to begin your hike.

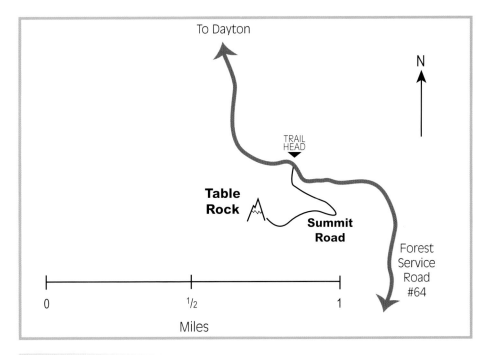

Summit Road
Starting Elevation: 6,047 Feet
Rating: Easy
Info: Pomeroy Ranger District
USGS topo map: Deadman Peak

After the bumpy, bone-jarring drive along Road 64, one should welcome getting out of the car and doing a little walking, and to reach the summit of Table Rock, only a little walking is needed. The summit road is in good shape and ascends moderately, taking you to the far end of the summit opposite your starting point. It's only a half mile, if that, to the top.

From the Summit

From Table Rock you'll have spectacular views of the Blue Mountains in every direction.

Looking roughly northeast, Oregon Butte (#34: 6,387 feet) can be seen. It's the high point on the second ridge system from where you stand, about 12 miles distant. If you have a pair of binoculars, you may be able to see the lookout cabin at its summit.

Looking just left of due south, the craggy, snow-capped Wallowa Mountain Range in Oregon can be seen, 60 to 70 miles away. If the day is clear, look to the left of the Wallowas in a westerly direction to see the Seven Devil Range in Idaho, 80 to 85 miles distant.

Looking westward, the patchwork quilt of Columbia Basin farms stretches beyond the Blues as far as the eye can see. The treed, green oasis is Walla Walla, 20 miles away.

A visit to Table Rock wouldn't be complete without a chat with the lookout personnel. There's plenty of interesting tidbits and anecdotes that only a person living atop a mountain for an entire summer could supply, and usually the lookout is glad to have visitors. However, don't assume he or she has no duties and can spend the whole afternoon talking, or that you can traipse into the lookout tower uninvited. This is the lookouts' private residence, and their time and dwelling should be respected.

U S Mountain

6,232 Feet

■ Round-Trip Length: **7 miles** ■ Elevation Gain: **832 feet** ■ Hiking Time: **4 hours**

A rough, four-wheel-drive road brings hikers close enough to the summit of U S Mountain in the Kettle Crest Range for a ten-minute off-trail hike to finish the climb. Though this hike is not as spectacular or wild as those of the surrounding higher peaks, it's a lightly used section of the Kettles that still provides great views of unspoiled forests.

With a wide trail and a vertical climb of a little more than 800 feet, this hike is a good choice for family hiking—long enough to gain a sense of accomplishment, yet not so demanding for children. The summit is treed, but open enough to allow views in all directions except to the north.

Getting There

■ From Kettle Falls, drive west on Highway 395 across the Columbia River. At the end of the bridge, turn left onto Highway 20 and drive 18.4 miles to graveled Albion Hill Road #2030.

■ Turn right and drive 7.6 miles to the unmarked trailhead on the right. You'll pass the marked Wapaloosie Mountain Trailhead, and then the Old Stage Road Trailhead, three-tenths of a mile beyond which is the U S Mountain Trailhead. It is a well-defined road with a brown marker barely visible among weeds and saplings at the right entrance. It is Road #600.

The Trail

Forest Service Road #600
Starting elevation: 5,400 feet
Rating: Break a Sweat
Info: Colville Ranger District
USGS topo map: Copper Butte

Though Road #600 is open to vehicles, it is seldom used. You'll likely run into no one on foot or otherwise during this hike.

Road #600 has its beginnings in a recent clear-cut. As you begin your hike, you'll see the road climbing steeply out of the clear-cut into a timber stand about a quarter mile ahead. Once you enter the wooded area, you'll stay under cover of trees for the entire hike save a few naturally open areas.

The road follows a broad-topped ridge for 3/4 of a mile after leaving the clear-cut with little change in elevation. Then the trail will begin climbing steeply, leaving the dense timber for open, grassy slopes. Soon the trail will level out as it skirts a subsidiary peak of U S Mountain about 45 minutes from the trailhead. The trail will descend the peak until reaching the saddle between the subsidiary peak and U S Mountain. At the saddle you can see a spring to the right that's fenced off with barbwire to prevent trampling by stock.

The road will ascend steeply again as it makes its final ascent of U S Mountain. But the road levels out and skirts to the left of the peak. Stay on the level section

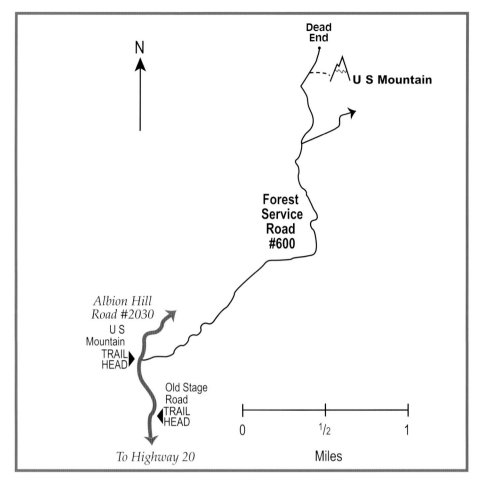

until it begins to descend steeply. At this point you'll see a very rough road leading to the right. Take it until it abruptly ends after about 50 yards. It leaves you on a rocky, open slope, allowing an easy ten-minute scramble to the summit.

From the Summit

Facing due west as you stand on the summit, you'll see a well-elevated ridge two miles away across the valley that's slightly fire-scarred at the top. The right end (north) with an almost imperceptible knob is Lambert Mountain. (#28: 6,525 feet). The high point of the ridge at the south end (left) is Midnight Mountain. (#21: 6,660 feet).

Looking to the northwest, a little over three miles away, the mountain to the right of Lambert and Midnight, also fire-scarred, and with open, grassy areas on its upper slopes, is Leona Mountain (#30: 6,474 feet).

Finding a spot that allows a view to the south, to the left of Midnight and Lambert Mountain, you'll see Copper Butte (#6 - 7,140 feet) three miles away with its open east-facing slope. Easily visible is Copper Butte's fire-devastated north slope, burned in 1994. The next mountain south of Copper Butte, four and a half miles from where you stand is Scar Mountain (#8: 7,046 feet). And beyond, just to the left of Scar's peak, you can see Wapaloosie Mountain. (#9: 7,018 feet) five and a half miles distant.

Linton Mountain

6,215 Feet

■ Round-Trip Length: **16 miles** ■ Elevation Gain: **3,035 feet** ■ Hiking Time: **10 hours**

A new trail constructed in 1995 brings hikers close to the summit of Linton Mountain, located northeast of Colville. The gently ascending trail makes the 3,000 foot elevation gain less strenuous than taking the old trail. But the price is a longer hike, and you'll need to get an early start if you don't want to arrive back at the trailhead after dark.

The new trail connects to an old, unmaintained trail that disappears short of the top. But the off-trail going is fairly easy through the open, subalpine landscape.

Linton is at the southern end of a ridge that connects to Abercrombie and Hooknose mountains, a pair of 7,000-footers. The scenery and views here are great, and it gets very light use. It's a good place to set up a backpacking camp to spend two or three days exploring.

Getting There

▓ Driving north on Main Street in Colville, turn right onto Third Street (Highway 20) and go 1.2 miles to the top of the hill.

▓ Turn left onto Aladdin Road and drive 25.4 miles until reaching a Y-intersection. Bear right and drive 7.3 miles, passing Deep Lake, until coming to graveled Silver Creek Road.

▓ Turn right and from here it's 4.2 miles to the trailhead.

▓ At six-tenths of a mile bear left at the three-way intersection marked with a sign reading "Gladstone."

▓ At 1.5 miles you'll cross a cattle guard, and the road becomes Forest Service Road 7078.

▓ At 1.9 miles the road forks. Bear right onto Road 070 and drive to the end of the road.

The Trail

South Fork Silver Creek Trail #123
Starting elevation: 3,180 feet
Rating: Major Workout
Info: Colville Ranger District
USGS topo map: Metaline

There are two trailheads at the end of Forest Service Road 070. Don't take the North Fork Silver Creek Trail #119 to Abercrombie Mountain. Trail #123 is across the stream, a little beyond the end of the gravel. A sign marks the trailhead.

Trail #123 starts out as an old logging road that follows the south fork of Silver Creek. The trailhead sign says its 3.8 miles to the end of the trail at Gunsight Pass. However, the actual distance is six to seven miles.

Twenty minutes into the hike the trail crosses the creek, then about five minutes later, re-crosses it. Shortly after the second stream crossing, you'll come to an unmarked fork. An old logging road veers left. The trail goes right, paralleling the creek. You can take either, but the trail is a bit shorter.

After another twenty minutes of walking, the trail and the old logging road come together again. At this point you can see the logging road crossing the stream to your right. This is the old South Fork Silver Creek Trail. You can cut your hiking time considerably if you take it. The road soon narrows into a trail, but you'll have an hour's steady grind up a very steep slope. The trail is overgrown in places and may be quite muddy if there's been recent rain. For a more moderate, but longer climb, turn left and take the new trail.

The new trail slowly ascends through a

thick forest of lodgepole pine. You can see occasional burned snags left from a huge fire that ravaged this area in the 1920s. The trail eventually levels out as it crosses onto a west-facing slope. Two and a half to three hours into your hike, you'll come to a spur trail on the right, also newly constructed in 1995, that goes about a quarter mile to a scenic overlook. From here you can see the valley below, along with a splendid view of Sherlock Mountain (#38: 6,365 feet).

Back on the main trail, continue for approximately thirty minutes more until the trail begins to switchback, descending to what seems like a channel cut between two hillsides. At this point you'll see a rough spur trail leading to the left. (If you miss it, you'll come to the end of the trail at Gunsight Pass after another five minutes of walking.) Take the spur trail for about 75-100 feet and you'll see another trail ascending to your left, cut deeply into the slope. This trail is unmaintained and overgrown. However, thanks to use by horsemen, it's well-defined and easy to follow. (Note: If you took the old South Fork Silver Creek Trail, it intersects the new trail near its terminus. Turn left and walk 3-4 minutes to the spur trail.)

The trail passes through thick undergrowth before breaking out and leveling on

an open ridge. It leads to a south-facing slope and begins to descend after passing some campsites. At this point you'll be able to see Mt. Linton up ahead for the first time. Continue following the trail as it bottoms out at the saddle and begins climbing the summit. About a quarter mile before the summit, the trail disappears and you'll have to bushwhack the remaining distance.

From the Summit

Looking roughly south, you can see a long stretch of the Pend Oreille River, as well as

A base camp can enable one to climb several mountains in two or three days.

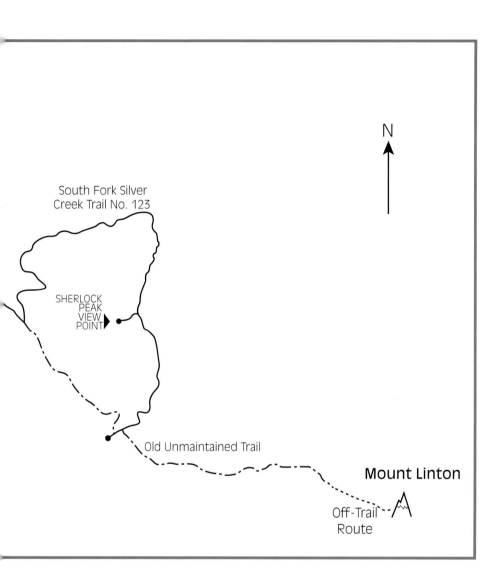

South Fork Silver
Creek Trail No. 123

N

SHERLOCK
PEAK
VIEW
POINT

Old Unmaintained Trail

Mount Linton

Off-Trail
Route

part of the town of Ione, about nine miles away. Looking almost due south, the prominent, rounded peak thirty miles distant is Calispell Mountain (#14: 6,855 feet).

Looking due west, the mountain across the valley, 2-3 miles away is Sherlock Mountain (#38: 6,365 feet).

Gazing due north, the higher-elevation mountain with the whitish, rocky summit, five miles distant is Hooknose Mountain (#4: 7,210 feet). A couple miles to the left of Hooknose, connected by a ridge, you'll see Abercrombie Mountain (#2: 7,308 feet).

Looking to the southeast across the Pend Oreille River valley, the high point thirteen miles distant with the twin, pointy peaks, is Molybdenite Mountain (#16: 6,784 feet)

If you hike to the subsidiary peak visible a quarter mile to the east, you'll be able to see the town of Metaline Falls in the valley below. Also visible above the town is the old limestone quarry and Mill Pond.

The body of water visible 2-3 miles to the south, adjacent to the power lines, is Lost Lake.

Mack Mountain

46

6,196 Feet
■ Round-Trip Length: **12 miles** ■ Elevation Gain: **746 feet** ■ Hiking Time: **6 hours**

The Kettle Range is chock full of mountains over 6,000 feet. However, the less prominent ones like Mack Mountain don't rate so high in recreational value. You won't find a trail to take you to Mack. Instead, there's a seldom-used four-wheel-drive road that brings you close to the summit. You may also run into cattle since the mountain is leased for grazing. Watch out for cow pies along the way.

With the trailhead at 5,450 feet, topping Mack Mountain requires an apparent vertical climb of only 746 feet. But it's not the case. This is a rather long hike that goes up and down like a roller coaster. Along the way you'll ascend the summit of #22 King Mountain at 6,634 feet, along with a couple other ridges that run perpendicular to the trail. The total elevation gain is probably closer to 2000 feet.

There are plenty of south-facing slopes with balds along the way, allowing great views. But the summit of Mack is flat and treed, offering no viewpoints.

Getting There
■ The trailhead for Mack Mountain is the same as #22 King Mountain. From Kettle Falls, drive west on Highway 395 across the Columbia River. At the end of the bridge, turn left onto Highway 20 and drive 18.4 miles to graveled Albion Hill Road #2030.
■ Turn right and drive 4.9 miles, passing the Deadman Creek Road turn-off and the Wapaloosie Mountain Trailhead.
■ There's no sign pointing out the Mack Mountain trailhead. It's on the right, consisting of two roads with a common starting point. Road #200 is the more obvious

road to the left. You want less-obvious Road #460, which is on the right. Both roads have markers indicating their numbers.

The Trail
Forest Service Road #460
Starting Elevation: 5,450 feet
Rating: Huffin' & Puffin'
Info: Colville Ranger District
USGS topo map: Copper Butte & Jackknife Mountain

Road #460 is a rough jeep road that begins by switchbacking uphill for the first thirty minutes of the hike. You'll reach the first of several ridgetops, descend a little, then begin climbing the next ridge. The second ridge takes less time to conquer though, and as you descend the other side, you'll be able to see King Mountain up ahead.

The saddle between the second ridge just climbed and King Mountain is a wide, flat, thickly-treed landscape of small-diameter lodgepole pine, 15-25 feet in height. As the road ascends King Mountain, it steepens as it approaches the summit. It does a switchback or two before delivering you at the summit. You'll immediately be able to see a rocky peak of

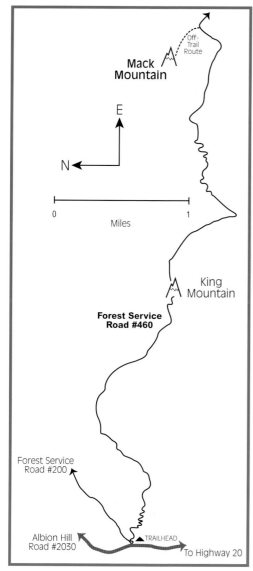

Mack Mountain

E

N

0   Miles   1

King Mountain

Forest Service Road #460

Forest Service Road #200

Albion Hill Road #2030

TRAILHEAD

To Highway 20

Off-Trail Route

peak to see Mack and its broad-topped, rounded summit lying to the east, about 500 feet lower in elevation than your vantage point.

Back at the fork, if you bear right, the road will soon descend steeply as it enters a south-facing bald. The steep portion will end when the road turns sharply toward the northeast and descends more moderately. Along this stretch, views of Mack Mountain with its treed summit and open, south-facing slope lying ahead are numerous. There are a couple rough roads along this section that intersect on the right that should be ignored.

There's a short, very steep downhill section when the road reaches the saddle between King Mountain and Mack Mountain. Then it roller-coasters up and down as it traverses Mack's open south slope. At any point along here, you can leave the trail and head upslope to reach the summit. However, the slope is quite steep. It's best to stay on the road until you reach Mack's southeastern side. The road here levels out, and will soon begin descending, your signal to turn off and head uphill. This slope is the most moderate approach, though you will soon have to traverse a timber stand with blowdowns. It's about fifteen minutes to the top after leaving the road.

From the Summit

It's hard to tell exactly where the highest point is on Mack. There are three small, ridgelike outcroppings of rock that run parallel with each other, separated by a distance of 30-40 feet. They all look about equal in height. But because the summit is so flat, any of the three could be the high point. Scramble across all three to insure that you've reached the top. This area is well-treed, so you won't have any views.

about equal height a half mile to the east. This is a subsidiary peak of King, a foot lower in elevation than the main peak. But from it, you can get a good view of your destination.

Continue on the road as it descends and follows a short ridgeline. Just short of reaching the subsidiary peak, the road forks. Bear right for Mack Mountain. But if you want the view, go left as the short road takes you near the top before ending. You'll have to stand at the east end of the

Taylor Ridge

6,190 Feet

■ Round-Trip Length: **7 miles** ■ Elevation: **1,105 feet** ■ Hiking Time: **4 hours**

Situated at the northern end of the Kettle Range, Taylor Ridge is a long, L-shaped ridge surrounded by hills and peaks thickly carpeted with evergreens. It gives a bird's-eye view of a sea of green that brings a sense of reverence and tranquility to the hiker that has huffed and perspired their way to the top.

A moderate-length trail will take you to the summit, but how long it'll last is anyone's guess. A large clear-cut near the beginning of the hike has caused a proliferation of grasses that is overgrowing the trail. This section is also leased for grazing.

However, once past the clear-cut, the hike to the summit passes through well-treed, remote forest that makes up for the ravaged lower portion of trail.

Getting There

■ From Kettle Falls, head west on Highway 395 across the Columbia River. At the end of the bridge, bear right and drive 16.7 miles north on Highway 395 to Boulder-Deer Creek Road where a sign reads, "Curlew 25 miles".

■ Turn left and drive 9.2 miles to graveled Forest Service Road #6113 marked with a sign that reads, "Bulldog Cabin".

■ Turn left and drive 9.1 miles of uphill gravel road until reaching a cattle guard. A few yards past the cattle guard, on the left, is a trailhead marker for the lower half of the Taylor Ridge Trail. Drive four-tenths of a mile past this trailhead to the start of the upper half of the trail.

■ The trail is marked by a weathered sign nailed to a tree on the right. Keep your eyes peeled, it's easy to miss.

The Trail

Taylor Ridge Trail #74
Starting elevation: 5,085 feet
Rating: Break a Sweat
Info: Colville Ranger District
USGS topo map: Mt. Leona

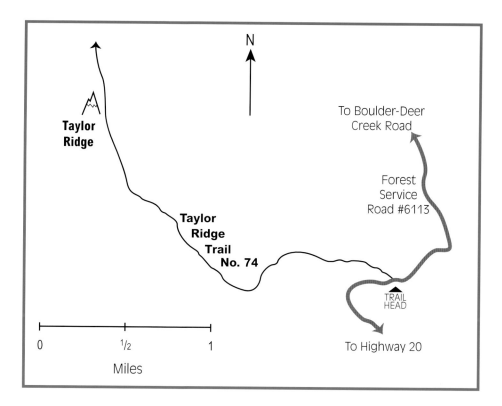

The trail begins by passing through a timber stand with numerous blowdowns before skirting, then entering a clear-cut. At the upper end of the clear-cut, the trail intersects an old logging road. Turn left and follow the road for 30-40 feet until the trail resumes again on the right.

Once you get past the clear-cut and the cowpie-littered range area, Taylor Ridge becomes a pleasant, pretty hike. You'll climb moderately through a forest of Douglas fir. In places the trail passes through open, grassy slopes and becomes indeciperable for short stretches, but if you continue on, it isn't hard to find again.

As you approach the top, the trail steepens. Just short of the summit, the trail is steepest as it goes directly up the slope without switchbacking. You can see a rocky butte ahead that marks the top. As the trail levels out, it goes past the rock outcropping to intersect with a road on the backside. Leave the trail and scramble to

the top of the outcropping to reach the high point of Taylor Ridge.

From the Summit
The view from here is impressive. The mountainous Kettle Crest, the low-lying Columbia River valley, along with forested slopes that are relatively free of clear-cuts, make Taylor Ridge a picturesque vantage point.

Many of the high peaks of the Kettle Range are visible to the south and southwest. The nearby peak, a little to the right of southwest, three miles away, is Profanity Peak (#32: 6,423 feet).

If you're up for more hiking, take the path to where it intersects a road just north of the summit. One can explore the entire ridge from this road. You'll find some old trailheads constructed back in the 1930s and 40s by the CCC that are no longer maintained. There's evidence of other CCC work if you poke around enough.

North Baldy Mountain

6,173 Feet
■ Round-Trip Length: **8 miles** ■ Elevation Gain: **1,353 feet** ■ Hiking Time: **5 hours**

I f you're looking for easy walking up a gentle slope, North Baldy is the mountain to choose. A road leading to the summit is passable by low-clearance vehicle to within a half mile of the top. But you can hike the entire summit road to get in a good dose of exertion without working up too much of a sweat.

If you don't mind walking on a road instead of a trail, and you can overlook the obvious signs of human intrusion into this area, you'll find this a pleasant hike. The landscape is a pleasing blend of thick woods, extensive grassy knolls, and rocky outcrops that tug at your desire to go off-trail and explore. And the 360-degree view from the top is outstanding.

Getting There
■ From Usk, cross the bridge spanning the Pend Oreille River and turn left onto LeClerc Road immediately after crossing.
■ Drive 13.4 miles to Forest Service Road No. 12 which is also marked Mill Creek Rd.
■ Turn right onto this gravel road and drive 10.2 miles, avoiding the numerous

less-traveled turn-offs, to the top of Pyramid Pass. The roadway is well-maintained gravel save the last 3-4 miles when it becomes a narrow, dirt road, though still passable by low-clearance vehicles.
■ At Pyramid Pass, which is marked by a sign, the road changes to Forest Service Road 312 and descends the other side. Park here and take the unmarked summit road on the left to North Baldy.

The Trail
North Baldy Summit Road
Starting Elevation: 4,820 feet
Rating: Break a Sweat
Info: Newport Ranger District
USGS topo map: North Baldy

From Pyramid Pass, take the dirt road on the left (heading north). The road gently inclines as it winds through the foothills leading to North Baldy. You'll have to walk about an hour before the mountain comes into view, but it'll be obvious—it's open south-facing slope is littered with rock outcrops, and there's an abandoned structure visible up top.

The summit road becomes steeper and rougher over the last three-quarters of a mile. It switchbacks shortly before terminating at the top.

From the Summit
Looking west, a long stretch of the Pend Oreille River is visible in the valley below. Looking across the valley, the high point a bit to the left of due west is Calispell Mountain (#14: 6,855 feet) about 18 miles distant. A couple ridges to the left of

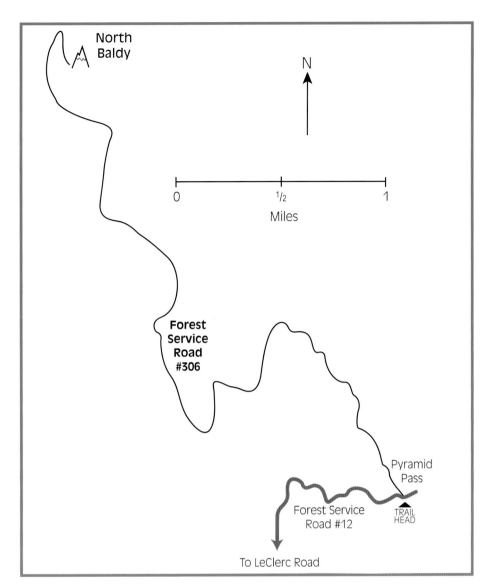

North Baldy

N

0   ½   1
Miles

Forest
Service
Road
#306

Pyramid
Pass

Forest Service
Road #12

TRAIL
HEAD

To LeClerc Road

Calispell, looking roughly southwest, the ski runs of 49 Degrees North Ski Area on Chewelah Mountain are visible if the day is clear.

Looking almost due south, the mountain with numerous clear-cuts on its lower slopes 8-9 miles distant, is South Baldy Mountain. Just to the right of South Baldy, approximately 43 miles distant, the twin humps of Mt. Spokane and Mt. Kit Carson are visible.

Looking northward, just left of due north, the pointed peak across the expansive valley, 12-13 miles distant, is Molybdenite Mountain (#16: 6,784 feet). Beyond Molybdenite, the many peaks of the Salmo-Priest Wilderness and the Canadian Rockies make an excellent backdrop.

And looking eastward, beautiful Priest Lake can be seen in the valley below. Beyond it, the many mountains of the Idaho Selkirks jut their pointy peaks skyward.

Seventeenmile Mountain

49

6,161 Feet

■ Round-Trip Length: **6 miles** ■ Elevation Gain: **1,811 feet** ■ Hiking Time: **5 hours**

This out-of-the-way mountain in the Kettle Range is so rarely hiked that it may go an entire summer without human visitors. The approach to Seventeenmile is a very pretty hike on a lightly-used, well-maintained trail.

Though the hiking time isn't long for this one, it requires about 1000 vertical feet of climbing without benefit of a trail. The going is steep, and in places, the route is thickly treed. But the rocky, open summit allows great views and a good place to hunker down for a respite after your arduous climb.

Getting There
■ From Kettle Falls, drive west on Highway 395 across the Columbia River, turning left at the end of the bridge onto Highway 20.
■ Drive 22.6 miles to the top of Sherman Pass, then continue down the other side an additional 9.9 miles toward Republic until reaching graveled Hall Creek Road. Turn left and from here the trailhead is 10.4 miles away.
■ Stay on Hall Creek Road, avoiding other turnoffs until coming to a fork at 5.3 miles. To the right is Nine Mile Road #2053. Don't take it, instead bear left onto Hall Creek Road #600.
■ Barely a mile further, the road splits again. Don't take Road 610 that goes left. Bear right and drive about four more miles to the trailhead, marked by a sign, on the right.
■ The last 4-5 miles of Hall Creek Road are narrow and occasionally rough. Though negotiable by low-clearance vehicles, you'll have to be careful in places.

The Trail
Thirteen Mile Trail #23
Starting elevation: 4,350 feet
Rating: Huffin' & Puffin'
Info: Republic Ranger District
USGS topo map: Seventeenmile Mountain

Thirteen Mile Trail heads west, terminating at Highway 21, a distance of 16.5 miles. But to reach Seventeenmile Mountain, you'll cover only the first 2.5 miles.

From the trailhead, the trail descends for a quarter mile before crossing a stream and climbing steeply up a knob. Atop the knob, about ten minutes into the hike, Seventeenmile Mountain comes into view. It's the rounded, treed mountain lying straight ahead as the path goes.

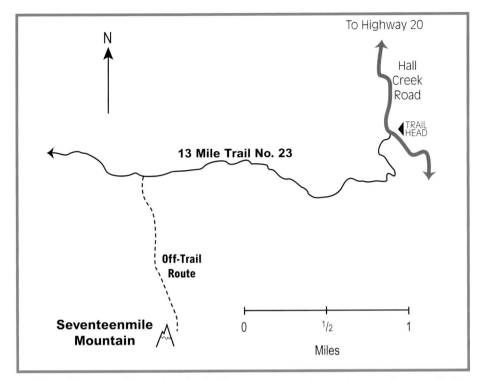

From here on, the well-maintained, easy-to-follow trail ascends. You'll pass by a section of huge, old-growth ponderosas, beside which you'll want to pause and admire. About an hour into the hike, the trail reaches its high point at the saddle between Fire Mountain which is on the right (north) and Seventeenmile Mountain, on your left (south). Looking west from here, you have a nice view of the Sanpoil River Valley, into which the trail descends. But at this point you'll want to turn left off the trail and head up the steep slope of Seventeenmile Mountain.

Though thickly treed, you can pick your way up the slope and have a clear route most of the way. Approaching the summit, small-diameter sub-alpine fir and Engelmann spruce grow thickly, and you'll have to push them aside as you barge your way to the top.

From the Summit

Upon reaching the summit, you'll find you came up the hard way—the south-facing slope is open and not as steep.

Looking due south about five miles distant, the rounded, logged mountain that looks about the same height is South Seventeenmile Mountain at about 5,840 feet. To the left of it, the mountain that's a little closer, with a summit that has a dip and a rocky protrusion in the middle, is Grizzly Mountain (#33: 6,397 feet)

Looking a little to the left of due east, the massive, broad-peaked mountain a little more than five miles across the valley is White Mountain (#12: 6,921 feet).

Following the ridge that extends north from White Mountain, the next hump is Barnaby Buttes (#27: 6,534 feet) six miles away. Looking to the left of Barnaby, you'll see the pointed summit of Bald Mountain (#11: 6,940 feet), also six miles distant. And from it, still going left, the final hump along the ridgeline, nearly due north from where you stand is Edds Mountain (#25: 6,550 feet).

6,161 Feet

■ Round-Trip Length: 6 miles ■ Elevation Gain: 1,321 feet ■ Hiking Time: 4 hours

The Kettle Range is the setting for this peak within hiking distance of the Canadian border. It's a fairly easy climb in an area managed primarily for cattle-grazing and timber production.

There's an old road to the summit that served a lookout dating from the 1930s. A four-wheel-drive vehicle can take you to the top. However the hike described here assumes you'll hoof it the entire length of the rough roadway.

Getting There

■ From the intersection of State Highways 20 and 21 near Republic, head north on Route 21 toward Curlew. Continue for 27.5 miles, passing Curlew until coming to signed Lone Ranch Creek Road. Turn right, immediately crossing the Kettle River.

■ Seven-tenths of a mile into graveled Lone Ranch Creek Road, you'll come to a fork. Bear right.

■ Four-tenths of a mile later is another fork. Bear left.

■ Drive an additional 2.8 miles to yet another fork. To the right is signed Forest Service Road #6120. Don't take it. Bear left onto unmarked Forest Service Road #668.

■ Just over one mile into Road 668, you'll cross a cattle guard and a sign notifies that you're on Forest Service Road #9576. From here the roadway cuts across steep hillsides as it climbs continuously.

■ Look for the third right turn, a little over five miles beyond the cattle guard. (The first two right turns are marked roads 9576-400. The third is unmarked.)

■ After the wide, right turn, the roadway is rougher and heads upward in the opposite direction that you've have been traveling. About a half mile into it, you'll come to a fork just after entering a clear-cut. Bear left, heading uphill. A couple tenths of a mile later you'll come to a berm preventing further travel unless you're driving a four-wheel drive. Park here and begin your hike.

The Trail

Unmarked Forest Service Road
Starting Elevation: 4,840 Feet
Rating: Break a Sweat
Info: Republic Ranger District
USGS Topo Map: Boundary Mountain

Start the hike by following the roadway on which you parked as it slowly ascends through a clear-cut. Fifteen minutes into the hike the road reaches a ridgecrest and levels out for a short distance. Expansive views to the north and east are possible here. However, at no point in the hike will you have a good view of Togo's summit.

■ *Togo Mountain*

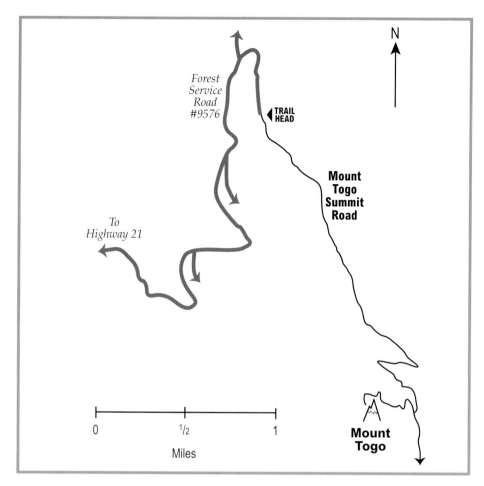

N

*Forest
Service
Road
#9576*

TRAIL
HEAD

**Mount
Togo
Summit
Road**

*To
Highway 21*

```
0          1/2          1
         Miles
```

**Mount
Togo**

A half hour into the hike you'll come to a fork. Bear right, heading uphill. From this point, the roadway is steeper and rougher.

The road switchbacks a couple times and about an hour into the hike reaches its highest point on Togo's slope where the summit road intersects on the right. Here an old sign pointing the way may be visible on the ground propped against a tree. The road descends from here, your signal to leave it and take the ascending summit road. Fifteen minutes of additional hiking will bring you to the top.

From the Summit

At the summit you'll find four concrete footings that supported the lookout that used to be here. Also, the remains of a pair of cabins can be seen.

Looking to the east, the two rounded summits close-by which appear to be higher are actually part of Mt. Togo. The second, more distant one is the highest point. It rises 129 feet higher than where you stand. It's heavily timbered and there's no trail, making a tough hike if you attempt to conquer it.

Looking in the distance to the southwest, the prominent, rounded mountain about 52 miles away is Moses Mountain (#18: 6,774 feet) on the Colville Indian Reservation. Looking just to the left of due west, the tall peak about 37 miles distant is Bonaparte Mountain (#3: 7,257 feet) in the Okanogan National Forest.

District Ranger Stations

For information about fee sites:

Northwest Forest Pass
1-800-270-7504
www.naturenw.org

Colville Ranger District
755 South Main
Colville, WA 99114
(509) 684-7000

Newport Ranger District
315 North Warren Ave.
Newport, WA 99156
(509) 447-7300

Republic Ranger District
P.O. Box 468
Republic, WA 99166
(509) 775-7400

Pomeroy Ranger District
Route 1 Box 53-F
Pomeroy, WA 99347
(509) 843-1891

Spokane Information Office
1103 North Fancher
Spokane, WA 99212
(509) 536-1200

Sullivan Lake Ranger District
12641 Sullivan Lake Road
Metaline Falls, WA 99153
(509) 446-7500

Tonasket Ranger District
1 West Winesap
Tonasket, WA 98855
(509) 486-2186

Walla Walla Ranger District
1415 West Rose Ave.
Walla Walla, WA 99362
(509) 522-6290

About the Author

James P. Johnson hiked and photographed
all fifty of the highest mountains in
Eastern Washington and enjoyed
every minute of it. He lives and
works in Spokane.

More Excellent Hiking and Outdoors Books!

COLOR HIKING GUIDE TO MT. RAINIER
Alan Kearney

As necessary as your backpack, this gorgeous, full-color hiking guide provides information on: access, weather, clothing, footwear, flora and fauna, supplies, photography tips, directions to and in-depth information on 30 different hikes. Alan has hiked all 215 miles of trails and shares his experiences, including round-trip mileage, elevation, and physical descriptions of each trail, with wildlife, indigenous plants, scenic highlights. 8 1/2 x 11inches, 72 pages.

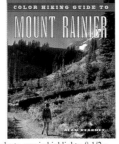

SB: $19.95 **ISBN: 1-57188-180-8**

COLUMBIA GORGE HIKES
Don and Roberta Lowe

Oregon's Columbia Gorge is one of the most gorgeous spots on the planet . Forty-two hikes covered, including hike length, elevation gain, high point, time needed, when open, and what you can expect to find along the way. 8 1/2 x 11 inches, 80 pages.

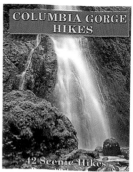

SB: $19.95 **ISBN: 1-57188-203-0**

DISCOVERING OREGON'S WILDERNESS AREAS
Donna Ikenberry

This all-color hiking guide features 100 of the finest walks found in Oregon's designated wilderness areas. Each wilderness is explained as to its history, outstanding features, accessibility. Hiking trails have been carefully selected for beauty and rated for exertion. Over 200 color photographs! 8 1/2 x 11 inches, 96 pages.

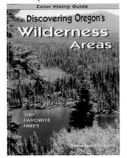

SB: $24.95 **ISBN: 1-57188-132-8**

HIKING MT. HOOD NATIONAL FOREST
By Marcia Sinclair

Oregon has been blessed with great natural beauty, one of its highlights is spectacular Mt. Hood and surrounding Mt. Hood National Forest. Less than one hour from downtown Portland, this natural wonder is a popular hiking destination. Marcia covers numerous hikes, what you can expect on each trail, including historical information and highlighting the flora and fauna you will experience along the way. 6 x 9 inches; 5 1/2 x 8 1/2; 130 pages.

SB: $19.95 **ISBN: 1-57188-271-5**

RAPTORS OF THE PACIFIC NORTHWEST
Thomas Bosakowski and Dwight G. Smith

Over the centuries, raptors have become both symbolic and metaphor for beauty, courage, swiftness, and above all, ferocity. In the U.S., raptors have been displayed as an emblem of strength, freedom, and power. *Raptors of the Northwest* features the following information on 35 species found throughout the Pacific Northwest: range; life history; behavior; conservation status; habitat requirements; nesting; eggs and young; hunting behavior and diet; territory and density; survey methods; conservation and management. 6 x 9 inches, 136 pages.

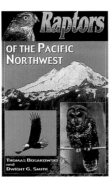

SB: $19.95 **ISBN: 1-57188-236-7**

PACIFIC NORTHWEST WEATHER
George R. Miller

The climate of the Pacific Northwest is as broad and varied as is found anywhere in the world—from dry eastern sections to cool and wet western regions. *Pacific Northwest Weather* explores the reasons for this, offering an in-depth look into those peculiarities specific to Pacific Northwest weather. Written and designed for the layperson, as well as a basic text in meteorology.

With interesting references to past storms, like the infamous Columbus Day storm, and weather patterns that cause heat waves and ice storms, this book has much to offer anyone interested in the weather. 8 1/2 x 11 inches, 170 pages.

SB: $25.00 **ISBN: 1-57188-235-9**

Ask for these books at your local outdoor store, bookstore, or order from:

1-800-541-9498 (8 to 5 P.S.T.) • www.amatobooks.com

Frank Amato Publications, Inc. • P.O. Box 82112 • Portland, Oregon 97282